SEMANTICS

of the WORLD

AFRO–LATIN AMERICAN WRITERS IN TRANSLATION

MARK A. SANDERS, SERIES EDITOR

Afro–Latin American Writers in Translation is a series of critical editions of celebrated works in translation aimed to advance research and academic reflection on the Black presence in Latin America and its influence across the Americas. By making Afro–Latin American writers more readily available to a North American audience, the works in the series will deepen our understanding of writing and race in New World history. The publications in the series will further provide a complementary critical history of the literary lives and the ever-evolving print cultures found across Afro–Latin American history and culture.

Semantics

of the World

selected poems

Rómulo Bustos Aguirre

Edited and Translated by

Nohora Arrieta Fernández and

Mark A. Sanders

University of New Mexico Press Albuquerque

© 2022 by the University of New Mexico Press
All rights reserved. Published 2022
Printed in the United States of America

ISBN 978-0-8263-6424-1 (paper)
ISBN 978-0-8263-6425-8 (electronic)

Library of Congress Control Number: 2022949499

Founded in 1889, the University of New Mexico sits on the traditional homelands of the Pueblo of Sandia. The original peoples of New Mexico—Pueblo, Navajo, and Apache—since time immemorial have deep connections to the land and have made significant contributions to the broader community statewide. We honor the land itself and those who remain stewards of this land throughout the generations and also acknowledge our committed relationship to Indigenous peoples. We gratefully recognize our history.

Publication of this book was made possible in part by a generous contribution from the University of Notre Dame

Cover image: bgwalkert | istockphoto
Cover designed by Mindy Basinger Hill
Interior designed by Isaac Morris
Composed in Adobe Caslon Pro 10 / 14

El mundo es siempre sí y no…

The world is always yes and no…

CONTENTS

Note on Translation	xiii
Rómulo Bustos Aguirre Chronology	xv
Acknowledgments	xvii
Introduction. Semantics of the World	xix

El oscuro sello de Dios / The Dark Stamp of God

Ícaro dudoso / Doubting Icarus	2 / 3
Hay alguien que yo sé morándome / I Know There's Someone Dwelling within Me	4 / 5
Cada día volvemos a inventar el paraíso / Every Day We Remake Paradise	6 / 7
Odiseo / Odysseus	8 / 9
Ajedrez / Chess Set	10 / 11
Jungla / Jungle	12 / 13
Socrática / Socratic	14 / 15
Palenqueras / Palenqueras	16 / 17
Monólogo del verdugo / Hangman's Monologue	18 / 19
Un hombre de piel negra / A Man with Black Skin	20 / 21

En el traspatio del cielo / On the Back Porch of Heaven

Árbol camajorú / Camajorú Tree	24 / 25
La visita / The Visit	26 / 27
Al otro lado del mundo / On the Other Side of the World	28 / 29
Matarratón / Matarratón	30 / 31
Crónica de la madre / The Mother's Chronicle	32 / 33
Crónica del mediodía / Midday Chronicle	34 / 35
Crónica de la hermana mayor / The Big Sister's Chronicle	36 / 37
Crónica de la noche / Night's Chronicle	38 / 39
Crónica del patio / Chronicle of the Courtyard	40 / 41
Vuelo y construcción del caballo de palo / Flight and Construction of the Hobby Horse	42 / 43
Crónica del árbol de agua / Chronicle of the Tree of Water	44 / 45
Poema de las pertenencias / Poem of Belongings	46 / 47

Poema a la hermana menor / Poem for the Little Sister   48 / 49
Balada de la casa / Ballad of the House   50 / 51
Palenquera / Palenquera   52 / 53

La estación de la sed / The Season of Thirst

Crónica / Chronicle   56 / 57
Cotidiano / Everyday   58 / 59
Ciempiés / Centipede   60 / 61
El pajarero / The Bird Catcher   62 / 63
Una vez en un sitio / One Time at the Spot   64 / 65
Botánica / Botánica   66 / 67
Cuento / Story   68 / 69
El don / The Gift   70 / 71
Escena de Marbella / Scene at Marbella   72 / 73
Destino / Fate   74 / 75
Epifanía / Epiphany   76 / 77
De la dificultad para atrapar una mosca / On the Difficulty of Catching a Fly   78 / 79
Monólogo de Jonás / Jonah's Monologue   80 / 81
El ángel / The Angel   82 / 83
Consejo / Advice   84 / 85
Orishas / Orishas   86 / 87

Sacrificiales / Sacrificials

Lo eterno / The Eternal   90 / 91
El carroñero / The Scavenger   92 / 93
Sicología de la madreperla / Psychology of the Mother-of-Pearl   94 / 95
Para un manual del inquisidor / For the Inquisitor's Manual   96 / 97
Mantarraya / Manta Ray   98 / 99
Poema con pez y garcetas / Poem with Fish and Egrets   100 / 101
Cotidiana / Everyday   102 / 103
Dactiloscopia / Dactyloscopy   104 / 105
De la levedad / Of Levity   106 / 107
Cinegética / Cynegetics   108 / 109

De los sólidos platónicos / Of the Platonic Solids	110 / 111
Contra Parménides o la mariapalito / Against Parmenides or the Little Stick Bug	112 / 113
El arcángel / The Archangel	114 / 116
Mirando una estampa de Santa Lucía en un texto hagiográfico / Looking at a Portrait of Saint Lucia in a Hagiographic Text	118 / 119
En el zoológico / In the Zoo	120 / 122
Sacrificial / Sacrificial	124 / 125
Un paco-paco / A Cricket	126 / 127
Poema probable / Probable Poem	128 / 129
La capa de juegos / The Magic Cape	130 / 131

Muerte y levitación de la ballena / Death and Levitation of the Whale

Cuento / Story	134 / 135
Observación hecha desde el hemisferio izquierdo del cerebro / Observation Made from the Left Hemisphere of the Brain	136 / 137
Del cangrejo ermitaño / Of the Hermit Crab	138 / 139
Euclidiano / Euclidian	140 / 141
De moscas y de almas / Of Flies and Souls	142 / 143
Para Wittgenstein / For Wittgenstein	144 / 145
Poiesis / Poiesis	146 / 147
Cenzontle / Cenzontle	148 / 149
Tropismos / Tropisms	150 / 151
Muerte y levitación de la ballena / Death and Levitation of the Whale	152 / 154
Evocando a G. Bateson / Evoking G. Bateson	156 / 157
El fulgor / The Radiance	158 / 159
Sufí / Sufi	160 / 161
Escalera / Stairs	162 / 163
Ilímites / Limitless	164 / 165
La casa / The House	166 / 168

La pupila incesante / The Incessant Pupil

Semántica del mundo / Semantics of the World	172 / 173
Ser y no ser / To Be and Not to Be	174 / 175

Jacob y el ángel revisitados / Jacob and the Angel Revisited	176 / 177
Metafísica / Metaphysics	178 / 179
Poeta / Poet	180 / 181
Poema de amor con serpientes, erizos y palomas / Love Poem with Snakes, Porcupines and Doves	182 / 184
Poema con sombra parlante / Poem with a Talking Shadow	186 / 187
Cabeza de Medusa con espejo / Medusa's Head with a Mirror	188 / 189
La pupila incesante / The Incessant Pupil	190 / 191
O viceversa / Or Vice Versa	192 / 193
Bertica / Bertica	194 / 195
Péndulo / Pendulum	196 / 197
Ceremonias / Ceremonies	198 / 199
Notes	201
Additional Reading	207
Works Cited	209

NOTE ON TRANSLATION

Nohora Arrieta Fernández and Mark A. Sanders

In the summer of 2016, we approached Rómulo Bustos with an idea for an English-language translation of his poetry. We think his poetry is wonderful, a gift to humankind, and therefore should be known beyond the Spanish-speaking world. He was elated by the idea and in a matter of weeks sent us his selections for the volume. He chose poems that best represent the concept and poetics for each of his major volumes: *The Dark Stamp of God, On the Back Porch of Heaven, The Season of Thirst, Sacrificials, Death and Levitation of the Whale,* and *The Incessant Pupil.*

At the same time, we devised a set of guidelines for translating Bustos's poetry that would make decisions consistent across the translation. Because Bustos is a poet of concision and understatement, we agreed to affect a comparable vocal style in English. Toward this end, we have employed an economy of words, simple diction, and whenever possible contemporary syntax, contractions, and the apostrophe (as opposed to "of") to form the possessive. However, there are exceptions. For example, when the verb "to be" needs greater emphasis, we have chosen not to use a contraction, or when the line needs to slow down (particularly toward the end of a poem), we use two words instead of the contraction for greater dramatic effect. The most consistent exception to these guidelines occurs in the poems in which Bustos himself is affecting a slightly elevated form of oration.

We have replicated, as closely as possible, Bustos's line breaks and spacing, allowing for some variation when the syntax in English requires it. Likewise, we have followed his pattern of capitalization at the beginning of lines, though the capitalized word in English may be different from its equivalent in Spanish, again due to changes in syntax. In terms of punctuation, Bustos's aesthetic is quite spartan in that he uses very few end stops and so allows lines to flow into one another, sometimes composing entire poems without punctuation. We have followed this approach meticulously.

Furthermore, we elected to annotate the volume lightly. The annotations explain references to Greek and Judeo-Christian mythology, flora and fauna specific to South America, and the few untranslated phrases. These annotations are by no means exhaustive; rather, we selected references that are most likely to be unfamiliar to North American readers, yet are essential to the understanding of the poem. Also, we have annotated words and phrases that remain in the original language (Aztec, French, or Latin) in the body of the original poem. Finally, we have left a few words and phrases in Spanish untranslated because they are the noun or title in reference to a thing that does not exist in the English-speaking world, or the word is a neologism and thus has no translation.

All translations are forms of interpretation; therefore, the translations that follow reflect our understanding of the original poems, hopefully interpretations that will encourage others. Toward this end, this volume is bilingual, offering the original followed by the translation so that readers may read the original Spanish, if possible, and English in conversation with one another, and offer their own translations and interpretations. In other words, we do not offer here a definitive translation, if such a thing exists, but the beginning of a conversation inspired and propelled by Bustos's artistry.

RÓMULO BUSTOS AGUIRRE CHRONOLOGY

1954	Born September 5 to Julio Alberto Bustos and Blanca Aguirre Arrocha in Santa Catalina de Alejandría, Colombia.
1963	The Bustos family moves to Cartagena.
1973–1980	Undergraduate studies at the Universidad de Cartagena.
1979	The first edition of *En tono menor* is published.
1985	Awarded National Poetry Prize from the Association of Coastal Writers.
1988	Publishes *El oscuro sello de Dios* (The Dark Stamp of God).
1990	Publishes *Lunación del amor* (Lunar Month of Love).
1991–1993	Master's studies in linguistics and Hispanic American literature at the Instituto Caro y Cuervo.
1993	Appointed professor of literature at the Universidad de Cartagena.
1993	Publishes *En el traspatio del cielo* (On the Back Porch of Heaven).
1993	Awarded the National Poetry Prize from the Colombian Institute of Culture.
1996	Publishes *Palabra que golpea un color imaginario* (The Word that Strikes an Imaginary Color).
1998	Publishes *La estación de la sed* (The Season of Thirst).
2004	Publishes *Oración del impuro* (Prayer of the Impure).
2007	Publishes *Sacrificiales* (Sacrificials).
2007	Awarded the Ausias Prize by the Colectivo de Crítica Poética, Addison de Witt (Addison de Witt Critical Poetics Collective) in Spain.
2008–2013	Doctoral studies in religion at the Universidad Complutense de Madrid.
2008	Publishes *De la dificultad para atrapar una mosca* (On the Difficulty of Catching a Fly).
2010	Publishes *Obra poética* (Poetic Works).
2010	Publishes *Muerte y levitación de la ballena* (Death and Levitation of the Whale).
2010	Awarded the Blas de Otero Poetry Prize from the Universidad Complutense de Madrid.
2010	Publishes *Doble fondo III* (Antología conjunta con el poeta venezolano Juan Calzadilla) (Twice as Deep III) with Venezuelan poet Juan Calzadilla.

2011	Publishes *El ángel insomne* (The Sleepless Angel).
2013	Publishes *La mirada de Orfeo* (A Glance from Orpheus).
2014	Publishes *Rómulo Bustos Aguirre: Poesía escogida* (The Selected Poems of Rómulo Bustos Aguirre).
2015	Publishes *Parábolas del vuelo* (Parabolas of Flight).
2016	Publishes *La pupila incesante: Obra poética 1988–2013* (The Incessant Pupil: Poetic Works, 1988–2013).
2017	Publishes *Casa en el aire* (House in the Air).
2019	Publishes *Monólogo de Jonás* (Jonah's Monologue).
2019	Publishes *La furia del cordero* (The Lamb's Fury).
2019	Awarded the National Poetry Prize by the Ministry of Culture.

Acknowledgments

With the publication of *Semantics of the World*, and thus the launch of the Afro–Latin American Writers in Translation series, we take another step toward the fuller assessment of Afro–Latin American writing and its central role in the politics, histories, and cultures shaping the Western Hemisphere. This step has been made possible by the collective efforts and inspiring generosity of so many family members, friends, colleagues, and institutions. Any success this volume may achieve is the direct result of their contributions, and all errors and shortcomings are entirely our own.

First and foremost, we thank Rómulo Bustos Aguirre for his artistry and support for this project. The world of art and ideas is infinitely richer because of his poetry.

Also, we would like to acknowledge our friends and family for their love and support.

Gracias a la familia Arrieta Fernández, a Gladys, Eduarda, Luisa Fernanda y Eduardo Andrés, por la confianza que sostiene. Gracias a las amigas y los amigos de la vida.

Thank you Arthrell Sanders and Isaiah Sanders for reading the early drafts of the introduction and giving us your honest reflections. And thank you Joshua Sanders for your words of encouragement. Thank you, too, Steve Saltzman and Susan Spencer for the kind of friendship, care, and advice that literally save lives.

As always, Lawrence Buell has been an inspiration, model, and guide through the choppy waters of academia. Thank you, Larry, for being there from the very beginning.

We remember and honor the late Rudolph P. Byrd. His love, insight, and vision saturate these pages. And the late Tony Dixon: we continue to carry him with us.

To our colleagues in the departments of Africana Studies and English at the University of Notre Dame, your enthusiasm and support for this project and the series in general have made so many things possible. Thank you so much.

And to our colleagues at Emory University—María Carrión, José Quiroga, and Karen Stolley—please know that you helped to plant the seeds for this project so many years ago.

Thanks too to Gwen Kirkpatrick, Joanne Rappaport, and Vivaldo Santos at Georgetown University for supporting this project in so many ways.

A number of institutions have supported this project both financially and otherwise. We owe a great debt of gratitude to the Fulbright Colombia office for introducing us and for the fellowships that helped to start this project.

Equally as important, thank you to Provost John McGreevy of the University of Notre Dame for providing the seed money to launch this series. And thank you Dean Sarah Mustillo, also of the University of Notre Dame, for your steadfast support of this scholarship.

Thank you, too, to Alison Rice and the Institute for Scholarship in the Liberal Arts (ISLA) at the University of Notre Dame. Your financial support for this project has been essential for its success.

And we extend a very special thanks to Paula Moreno and the Biblioteca Afro-Colombiana. This project would have been impossible without your advice and the example of the Biblioteca.

Also, we would like to thank everyone who helped to edit and prepare this manuscript. Thank you to Peyton Davis for your detailed and accurate annotations. And to Laura Coll Pizarro and Sara Judy, thank you for such sharp editing of the early drafts of these translations. Thank you too to the outside readers for your insightful comments and for saving us from more than one embarrassing mistake. Also, Juan David Salas, thank you for ensuring the accuracy of our endnotes.

Finally, we offer a heartfelt thanks to Michael Millman, James Ayers, Norman Ware, and the entire University of New Mexico Press staff for editing and designing such a beautiful volume and for supporting the Afro–Latin American Writers in Translation series.

INTRODUCTION

SEMANTICS OF THE WORLD

Nohora Arrieta Fernández and Mark A. Sanders

... man is condemned to be free.
—*Jean-Paul Sartre, "The Humanism of Existentialism"*

Rómulo Bustos Aguirre grew up in a house full of books. On September 5, 1954, Julio Alberto Bustos and Blanca Aguirre Arrocha bore the last of their thirteen children, a boy who quickly became a voracious reader like his parents. As the story goes, Julio Alberto, a librarian, took two shelves full of his own books from his house to found the first public library in Rómulo's hometown, Santa Catalina de Alejandría,[1] a small town equidistant between Cartagena and Barranquilla along the Caribbean coast of Colombia. And although the family was of modest means, Julio Alberto provided books for all of his children. His son, Rómulo, recalls sitting in the courtyard of his small house reading Spanish translations of Edgar Allan Poe, Robert Louis Stevenson, Nathaniel Hawthorne, and Herman Melville, the works of Jorge Luis Borges and Héctor Rojas Herazo, and Greek and Roman mythology. Surrounded by fruit trees—mangos, mamoncillo, and tamarinds—taking in their intoxicating aromas and tasting their sweet fruits, Bustos often reflected on the lone *camajorú* tree that would become archetypical in his poetic recollections of childhood. There, on the "back porch of heaven," the furtive imagination of the precocious child could romp with gods and monsters, invent fantastic creatures, and even glimpse the divine. As we will see, youth, memory, and the courtyard would become overarching themes in Bustos's poetry, combining to celebrate the sacred while contemplating its passing, or perhaps to articulate the romantic yet ultimately vain attempt to suture that originating wound separating humankind from the knowledge of itself.[2]

When Bustos was nine, the family moved to Cartagena in search of greater educational opportunities for the children. As a result of the move, Bustos was able to attend high school and subsequently the Universidad de Cartagena, where he studied law and political science. There, he became involved with the En tono menor group, a gathering of idealistic students critiquing and protesting the rigidity and provincialism of the Colombian culture of his young adulthood. This group of budding intellectuals included the historian Alfonso Múnera, the prose writer Pedro Badrán, and the poet Jorge García Usta, who would later influence the development of Bustos's poetry. Bustos and Múnera would go on to contribute to the founding of the College of Humanities and the Department of Literature at the Universidad de Cartagena, where Bustos still teaches.

Bustos is the author of ten major collections of poetry: *El oscuro sello de Dios* (The Dark Stamp of God), 1988; *Lunación del amor* (Lunar Month of Love), 1990; *En el traspatio del cielo* (On the Back Porch of Heaven), 1993; *Palabra que golpea un color imaginario* (Word that Strikes an Imaginary Color), 1996; *La estación de la sed* (The Season of Thirst), 1998; *Sacrificiales* (Sacrificials), 2007; *Obra poética* (Poetic Works), 2010; *Muerte y levitación de la ballena* (Death and Levitation of the Whale), 2010; *La pupila incesante: Obra poética 1988–2013* (The Incessant Pupil), 2016; and *Casa en el aire* (House in the Air), 2017. As a result of his burgeoning body of exceptional work, Bustos is one of Colombia's most celebrated writers, having garnered numerous awards, including the National Poetry Prize from the Association of Coastal Writers (1985), the National Poetry Prize from the Colombian Institute of Culture (1993), and the Blas de Otero Poetry Prize from the Universidad Complutense de Madrid (2009).[3] As further evidence of Bustos's national prominence, *Obra poética*, an anthology of previously published poems, was published as a part of La Biblioteca de Literatura Afrocolombiana (the Afro-Colombian Library), a nineteen-volume collection of literary works by Colombia's most noted Black writers. And most recently, he was awarded the 2019 National Poetry Prize by the Ministry of Culture.

Critics most often describe Bustos as a metaphysical poet, preoccupied with essences and the existential, and he himself claims the label when commenting on the relationship between exteriority and interiority, one of his proxies for the paradox of existence:

> In reality, I am talking about my interiority, about the most intimate and secret requirements of my interior being.... I am talking about the relation between my interiority and another outside ... [i]n a certain sense, a metaphysical outside. For this I no doubt affirm that from a certain perspective my poetry is metaphysical.[4]

But what does it mean for a Black poet from a family of limited means on Colombia's northern coast to claim this mantle? For a North American audience, the label seems to reference the celebrated seventeenth-century English poets—John Donne, George Herbert, Andrew Marvell, Richard Crashaw, and others—best known for what was then a new angular poetics. Taking up a "shared awareness of the inter-relationship between the life of man and the universe,"[5] these poets employed juxtaposition, an economy of language, jarring conceits, rough versification, new verse forms, and other techniques in order to pursue what we now understand as fundamental existential questions. Not unlike our own moment, their era confronted the failure of Christianity and/or Greco-Roman philosophy and ethics to keep pace with science and to explain the palpable and phenomenological world that continued to change ever more rapidly.

However, to limit Bustos's invocation of the metaphysical to seventeenth-century British literature does not fully address the geopolitical position of a Black Colombian poet writing at the turn of the twenty-first century. When Bustos uses the term "metaphysical," he is not simply invoking Donne and others as literary progenitors; instead, he is laying claim to a much broader constellation of ideas, literary approaches, more immediate (and local) literary forebears, and Black geopolitical spaces to define his cultural/historical moment and help in deciphering it.

As mentioned earlier, Bustos concerns himself with the nature of existence at the turn of the twenty-first century—humankind's relationship to itself and the universe, the meaning or purpose, if any, of human existence, and the daunting task of discerning that meaning. Where earlier epistemologies have failed to address these concerns fully, poetry, as far as Bustos is concerned, must stand in the breach, offering a means of confronting the "mystery," as he puts it, and at moments to see it more clearly, if not understand it more profoundly. Addressing the fundamental role of poetry, Bustos comments:

> The multiple forms of knowledge all share the same root: the human need to transform a sense of the complexity of being in the world. Therefore, religion, philosophy, poetry (even science) revolve around the same wound: humankind faced with the mystery. Reality is always elusive, opaque, and mocking before man's pretensions to reduce it to his own scale. His only defense is imagination.... While religion, theology, and philosophy derive from dogma or closed systems that suffocate, the poetic imagination is the opening that makes way for more openings. It doesn't try to reduce reality; it seeks to follow its dance steps.[6]

In a way, Bustos sees his poetry as a response to the modern burden of "freedom," in Jean-Paul Sartre's sense of the term—the daunting task of creating or choosing the value or meaning that would explain our existence. Such a burden often results in solitude, despair, and profound alienation; the failure to create meaning or a recognition of the absurdity of the task is an omnipresent risk. Indeed, Bustos's speakers perpetually struggle to construct, assign, or discern meaning in a world of relentless opacity, just as the poet himself works to create a poetic language capable of conceptualizing the compelling paradox at the heart of modern life.

Lázaro Valdelamar Sarabia calls this crisis "existential orphanage."[7] Thus, Bustos's poetry seeks to suture the originating wound or separation by reimagining childhood, nature, and supernatural beings (angels, for example) as a means of returning to a state of wholeness. Or through irony, skepticism, and doubt, Bustos asserts the utter impossibility of reunification or return.

Emiro Rafael Santos locates this crisis in language and thus understands Bustos's poetry more as a linguistic project, the poem and poet in the process of reconstructing a heretofore debilitated language. If language can no longer name and assign meaning, as in the failed Greco-Roman or Judeo-Christian mythic traditions, then the poet must stress the poem itself as the process of reconstruction. For Santos, the poem does not simply disrupt the traditional narratives and their implicit epistemologies but raises the question of knowledge itself, particularly in relation to the semiotic systems normally used to create it:

> Bustos Aguirre builds an ironic, metaphoric system of thought in which symbols are put to work, with all their historical and cultural weight, to renew the linguistic materiality of which they are a part. Since the inert symbols and concepts deny the dynamism of the world, the poem must become the event that allows the names to be renamed.[8]

As mentioned earlier, Bustos's philosophical poetics emerge from a lifetime of voracious reading. His immersion in nineteenth-century US writers, particularly Herman Melville, Walt Whitman, and Robert Louis Stevenson, gave him an expansive sense of romance and nearly unlimited possibility. Furthermore, Bustos reiterates the importance of Poe in his artistic development, the fantastic and the phantasmagoric in relation to the tortured soul. Greek philosophy is equally as important; Socrates, Parmenides, Plato, and Aristotle in particular have informed Bustos's approach to epistemology and ontology, while Greek mythology has helped to shape his understanding of the relationship between language, myth, and meaning. For Bustos, "the great myths illuminate a primordial cartography of being, a dramatic cartography of the soul. It is exactly there where poetry begins."[9]

In a Latin American context, Luis Carlos López (a native son of Cartagena), Gabriel García Márquez, Jorge García Usta, Rubén Darío, Pablo Neruda, Octavio Paz, Jorge Luis Borges, and Héctor Rojas Herazo have had a discernible impact on Bustos's poetry. Of this group, Borges and Herazo have played dominant roles—Borges for his relentless questioning of reality and his willingness to reimagine it, and Herazo for the ways in which he correlates geography with emotional states. Indeed, Bustos wrote an essay on Herazo's presentation of the Caribbean in which he focuses on "the profound relationship between the enigma of being and geography" in Herazo's fiction.[10] "It is central to this dialogue," Bustos writes, "this intensely subjective impulse—one derived from imbibing that geography, that culture, this history... to build his vision of man and the Caribbean."[11] For Bustos, the most important geographic space is the courtyard, a point to which we will return shortly.

All modernists of one stripe or another, these writers provide concepts and structural models that manifest themselves in Bustos's poetry. In a formal sense, Bustos writes entirely in free verse, a direct result of Rubén Darío's innovations. Prior to Darío's poetry, Spanish poetics (either peninsular or Latin American) had languished in the wake of the Golden Age; by the end of the nineteenth century these poetics, and the Spanish language by extension, lacked the vitality, suppleness, and range commensurate with the rapid and raucous change of European and American modernism. Thus, somewhat analogous to the ways in which Walt Whitman transformed North American poetics, Darío almost singularly reinvented Latin American poetics. As Octavio Paz points out, by taking full advantage of "rhythmic versification" and introducing new voices, Darío paved the way for the use of free verse and the prose poem, effectively resurrecting a modernist poetics capable of exploring a new "way of looking at the world, a way of feeling it, knowing it, and speaking it."[12] Fast on Darío's heels, Pablo Neruda, Octavio Paz, and César Vallejo further advanced the reinvention of a modern poetic language that could ultimately provide for the existential musings that would define Bustos's poetry.

More specifically, Bustos is a poet of concision and compression, deploying a poetics of economy that exacts particular pressure on each word while pointing up the spaces or silences between words. What goes unsaid is almost as important as what is said, silence bearing weight just as sound does. In this sense, Bustos's sense of understatement complements his philosophy, in which the play between silence and sound, absence and presence, underscores a posture of both wonder and doubt. This impossible duality, the *both/and* of his poetry, emanates from an enduring ambivalence over the power or limitations of the "mythopoetic," as he terms it, either to heal and recover or to proclaim the utter impossibility of recuperation. Finally, it is this perpetual play between seemingly irreconcilable opposites that drives his poetics and defines his overarching aesthetic.

A way of grounding the theoretical and philosophical in a strategy of reading and interpretation is to think of Bustos's poetry in terms of four overlapping concepts: paradox, physical space, nature, and mythology. In terms of paradox, for Bustos, seeming contradictions lead to more probing questions that may point toward revelation, or at least better register the *both/and* at the heart of his existential project. For example, silence, as mentioned earlier, serves as a recurring concept relative to paradox. In an interview with Emiro Santos García, Bustos comments:

> In reality, poetry needs a language for naming silence. To name, better yet, to besiege silence. If one could name it, silence would no longer really be silent. . . . Silence is irreducible to the word. In this incessant battle and wasteland, we can find poetry. This paradox of language and silence serves as the foundation of poetry; better yet, it is the poem itself.[13]

For Bustos, the language of poetry must do the impossible, name that which by definition cannot be named, and thus Bustos writes poems that explore the mystery of this dilemma. Note how "One Time at the Spot" (from *The Season of Thirst*) dramatizes the play between sound and silence.

One Time at the Spot

One time at the spot
I saw this guy dancing
        with his eyes closed
his feet barely touched the ground
His skin was dark and beautiful
without a single mark
So I said to myself:
How long will his dance last?

Here, a man dances in a state of near ecstasy, a state in which the speaker and the reader can participate vicariously. As both luxuriate in the sensuality of the scene, the poem turns to question the temporal dimension of the moment. Ending with the line, "How long will his dance last?," the poem ponders what, if anything, will follow this scene. What is the meaning of the silence that follows the sound, the stasis that follows motion, the death that follows life? For Bustos, this question is the very stuff of poetry.

In a similar sense, "Chronicle" (also from *The Season of Thirst*) offers silence and emptiness as enigmatic responses to a mother's gesture of protection and care.

Chronicle

Just a few days after I was born a demon appeared
He passed over the bed's headboard
following the movement of my eyes with his beak
Once again
mother scares him with a cry in the middle
                            of a memory
then adds with a smile
"now you would be blind, my son"
"yes, mother"—I say
staring at the empty horizon

Here, the boy's empty stare signals a silence or indeterminacy that leaves open the meaning of the mother's protection or her smile. Has the boy lost his sight, and what is the meaning of his stare into the "empty horizon"? Does the poem bring us to the brink of existential crisis? What is not said here? Note the lack of punctuation, particularly at the end of the poem—a technique he uses in many of his poems. This lack of punctuation often leaves the reader largely on their own to discern units of meaning; they must perpetually construct or reconstruct the poem in order to assign it coherence. So too, absent guiding punctuation, the unit of time (and its meaning) between words and phrases remains ambiguous. Even the ending of the poem is in doubt, thus playing up the relationship between sound and silence in the creation or perpetual re-creation of the poem.

    Analogous to silence, the play between inside and outside, interior and exterior also serves as a register for paradox. For example, "Jonah's Monologue" (also from *The Season of Thirst*) recasts the Hebrew Bible myth of Jonah and the whale, as a story not so much about obedience and prophecy but about the fictional border between the self and the cosmos. Captive in the belly of the beast, as it were, Jonah is free to contemplate an intimacy or connectedness he did not otherwise know existed: "Sometimes it confuses me the ferment of his breathing / the vibration of his heartbeat magnified by its echo / . . . Perhaps I am the whale's heart." If we are all but stardust, mere far-flung remnants of some long-dead supernova; if we are all made of the same elements, then what is the difference between Jonah and the whale's heart, between humankind and nature, the individual and the cosmos? At this point, the lines of demarcation normally used to order the palpable world disappear; indeed, these artificial barriers give way to a more expansive and disorienting contemplation of existence and meaning. If, in the end, Jonah is the whale's heart, do Jonah and/or the whale cease to exist as such? What is the meaning of *Jonahness* or *whaleness* if there's no difference between the two?

For Bustos, the play between inside and out, center and periphery serves as an occasion to contemplate the collapse of boundaries or borders that prop up outmoded epistemologies, ones that prevent the fullest exploration of the modern existential state. For example, "Jungle" (from *The Dark Stamp of God*) asks what happens when external threats become constitutive elements of the self.

Jungle

The jungle doesn't reside only
in the tiger's heart, or in his claws
The menacing air, the roar, the dark
horror, the bite
these hang on the left side of your chest
        like an innocent medallion
Any day
you pick up the mirror
you could be the first victim

The jungle, that menace where humans can easily fall prey to animals truly at the top of the food chain, does not exist simply as a remote location rarely to be encountered. "The lion's heart," "his claws," or "the bite" do not exist outside of ourselves but serve as an essential part of our emotional and psychological makeup. This seemingly remote threat is a part of us, a perpetual threat that confronts us each time we look in the mirror. Here, what is beyond the self and a part of the self become one and the same. This dissolution of the boundary between inside and out, the individual and the physical world, the self and the cosmos serves as one of the hallmarks of Bustos's poetics. In a larger sense, paradox—here the dependent relationship of opposites, sound and silence, inside, and outside, and so on—offers a means of knowing beyond established paradigms, a way of questioning and discovering foreclosed by the systems of thought that created the very oppositions.

If paradox serves as Bustos's strategy for exploration, geography provides the site, the physical space that offers both the occasion for exploration and an objective correlative—an emblem or emotional register for the philosophical challenge. As mentioned earlier, Héctor Rojas Herazo plays a large role in Bustos's approach to poetics and place; in particular, his novels *En noviembre llega el arzobispo* (The Archbishop Arrives in November) and *Verano* (Summer), and poems such as

"Tránsito de Caín" (Cain's Passing) and "La noche de Jacob" (Jacob's Night), explore the correlation between space and psychic or emotional states. Certainly, this correlation is not new, but Bustos finds in Herazo the exploration of this correlation specific to the Caribbean, or put slightly differently, the assertion of the Caribbean as a site of existential doubt and reflection.[14]

For Bustos, the specific site of the back porch, courtyard, or backyard (depending on how one might translate "traspatio") serves as a geographical space of existential reflection. Indeed, Bustos's third collection is titled *On the Back Porch of Heaven* and includes a poem with the same title. Invariably, poems that feature the space of the *traspatio* begin as reflections on childhood, and with a child's sense of imagination and wonder often entail vibrant colors, pungent aromas, and a natural landscape commensurate with a child's capacity for wonder—a point to which we will return shortly. Lázaro Valdelamar Sarabia provides a cogent reading of this space:

> The courtyard serves as a sacred center for the poetic "I"; it is nocturnal and the matrix, affirming the ties with the original point from which it springs and around which life as a whole coheres.
>
> This harmonious space in the unconscious is populated with fruit trees, the brothers with their games and above all, by the mother. Also, there is a being that symbolizes the harmony between that world and its source, a child angel.[15]

An instructive example of Bustos's approach to space is "The Visit" (from *On the Back Porch of Heaven*)—a poem that takes up the tamarind tree in the backyard of his youth. An angel asks for "dulce de tamarindo" (a candy made from the fruit of the tamarind tree), then stains her shirt with the juice from the camajorú tree's fruit. The speaker tells her how to clean her shirt in order to avoid a scolding from her mother.

As Sarabia points out, the scene provides a unity of the divine and human worlds. Here the child angel, perhaps a reference to the poet himself, eats the tamarind tree's fruit, food for the gods. So too, the tree serves as a "scale toward the absolute,"[16] a symbol of the united realms of the divine and the human. To underscore the point, the poem ends reflecting on the tree's fruit on the ground: "Outside it looked as though there had fallen to the ground / The most magnificent asteroids." Thus, the courtyard serves as the site at which the individual may encounter the divine.

So too, "The Chronicle of the Courtyard" (also from *On the Back Porch of Heaven*) delivers a scene of a commonplace accident as it gives way to the contemplation of essences. As the story goes, the women in the courtyard shelling rice have spilled their day's work. And though the courtyard may seem indifferent to the waste—its ghostly silence—the moon spills out its light in kind. As a result, the natural world is transformed; "the rocks, the palm, the fence of sticks" transmogrify to reveal their essences, to become truly "rarified" things. Perhaps the moon imbues both human labor and the natural world with a touch of the divine.

As we have seen, the geographic space always references the natural world, either as a sign of the connection between the palpable world and the divine, or as a site of existential doubt, or both. In terms of the former, "Camajorú Tree" (also from *On the Back Porch of Heaven*) presents this iconic tree in the backyard of Bustos's youth as an *axis mundi*, as Sarabia argues,[17] growing in two directions, toward heaven and the center of the earth. Part I establishes the divine implications of the tree.

Camajorú Tree

I

Way back in the backyard
Past the mango, past the sleeping plum
there is a lone tree, the solitary camajorú
surrounded by thirst,
once the heavens opened up
in a beam of light and held the tree transfixed
We looked at it from afar
But we can no longer see its branches.
                        They're invisible
They flew high. And there they remained
                    held way up above us
And they are now the roof of the world

The tree makes up the "roof of the world," the sky, as it were, which in Spanish is *cielo*, meaning both sky and heaven. Part II describes the tree's roots as they grow "down / like the steps in a dream," and the tree's fruit, which can cause blindness but also provides sustenance for the angels. Ultimately, the poem "semantically articulates 'the theme of the backyard,'" according to Sarabia, "in terms of the search for the sacred." Thus, the angel and the tree return the search for the absolute to the previous and miraculous time of childhood.[18]

At the same time, "Camajorú Tree" represents Bustos's ongoing exploration of existential doubt. For Bustos, the natural world is not limited to the courtyard but can encompass practically all of nature, and the cosmos as well. Poems such as

"Matarratón," "Night's Chronicle," "Chronicle of the Tree of Water," "Centipede," "Story," "Fate," "Of the Difficulty of Catching a Fly," "Jonah's Monologue" (as we have already seen), "The Scavenger," "Against Parmenides or the Little Stick Bug," "In the Zoo," "To the Cricket," "Of the Hermit Crab," "Death and Levitation of the Whale," "Limitless," and so many more, vacillate between the wonder Bustos's speakers find in the natural world and its utter inscrutability. Or better yet, the poems offer the natural world, where in one sense existential angst might be allayed, if for just a moment, and in another the natural world serves as the correlative itself for the void, the mystery, the originating wound.

For instance, "Limitless" (from *Death and Levitation of the Whale*) offers an unapologetically romantic vision of a horse galloping. The descriptions of the horse's suspended hooves and the four petals of the rose combine to deliver a moment of transcendence: "For an instant / the animal is a bird," a horse in flight with all of the implications of flight—transportation, transformation, revelation, escape, deliverance, and limitless potential—that the Western romantic tradition assigns it.

Yet a poem such as "Of the Difficulty of Catching a Fly" (from *The Season of Thirst*) expresses a greater sense of ambivalence or doubt over any enduring meaning the natural world may offer.

On the Difficulty of Catching a Fly

The difficulty of catching a fly
lies in the complicated composition of its eye

It's more like the eye of God

Across a network of little eyes
it can see you from every angle
always ready to flee

It looks like the fly's one big eye
doesn't distinguish between colors

And it probably doesn't distinguish between you
       who are trying to catch it
and the rest of the garbage it's sitting on

In a radical revision of Judeo-Christian-based epistemology that places humankind at the center of god's creation, the poem first elevates the fly to the status of a god, then reduces the position of humankind to that of an impotent bystander, no more significant than a pile of trash. The pan-optical power of the fly's eye makes the fly more powerful than the reader, and to the extent to which the reader would want to catch and kill the fly, its powerful eye makes this attempt to reassert humankind's preeminence that much more difficult. Furthermore, "to catch," also means to comprehend the fly and all that it signifies in terms of humankind's impotence and ultimate irrelevance. This kind of comprehension becomes that much more difficult because few wish to accept such a revelation.

In a similar sense, in "The Scavenger" (from *Sacrificials*), Bustos offers this heretofore discredited or "dirty" animal as a possible image of god. Here, the animals that eat carrion or excrement (or both)—vultures, crows, hyenas, opossums, coyotes, Komodo dragons, worms, and so on—deliver, through digestion and defecation, new life: "In an odd way / the scavenger also works to resurrect / the dead." Again, alleged opposites are codependent: life and death. But does this vision of resurrection hold out hope or meaning for humankind? In the face of this poem and Bustos's larger vision, the myths that gave meaning to life in previous centuries literally fail under the weight of the poet's scrutiny.

In an interesting, perhaps predictable turn, Bustos also bends this line of reflection toward his own poetics, extending the existential reflection on the meaning of his poetry. For example, "Of the Hermit Crab" (from *Death and Levitation of the Whale*) compares the peripatetic habits of the hermit crab to the poet's search for meaning. That the hermit crab continually inhabits new spaces, first making them home, then abandoning them, suggests an essential restlessness in humankind—"the secret hermit crab that lives / in each one of us." It is that restlessness that perhaps creates poetry, a perpetual search for meaning or "home"; yet in its essential state of unrest, it suggests that meaning or home may remain out of reach.

Perhaps the title poem of the collection, "Death and Levitation of the Whale," best combines these dueling impulses. In a dreamlike state, the speaker imagines the descent of a dead whale into the abyss of the deepest ocean. First, the sheer immensity of the animal strikes the speaker: "230 tons of carrion or food falling / 230 worlds of gravity pushing toward the bottom / 230 infinite tons of vertigo." While commenting on the process of desolation, the speaker also ponders whether the whale is falling or the abyss is rising: "How do you know with certainty if a body's falling / on the world / or if it's the world that's rising/

falling / to the said body?" This paradox recurs throughout the poem, strongly suggesting the inscrutable nature of the scene. What ultimately is the nature of falling? How do we know what it is and what it means?

Maybe the meaning lies in the contemplation of the whale itself; this "Terrible, white whale" may hold the key to "the abyss, in the vast / magnificence of the void." Or perhaps it is the enigma of the whale that reflects the enigma of knowing. Within a dream, whose attachment to reality is already in question, a dead whale both falls and rises, decays and is reborn. As its descent is both awesome and terrifying, the dream is both a wonder and a nightmare. Finally, "this mysterious place where the whale / could also see us falling or ascending in a hazy dream" may well be the very limit of knowing, the place where the process of existential reflection can only turn back on itself in perpetual and meaningless repetition.

This simultaneous possibility of meaning and meaninglessness perhaps finds its most explicit expression through Judeo-Christian and Greco-Roman mythology. For Bustos, both provide systems of thought for contemplating or encountering the super real, supplying angels, chimeras, and other mythic creatures to consider god's conspicuous absence or possible death. As suggested earlier, Bustos is very much preoccupied with the fantastic, and with the dissolution of the fictive boundaries between the palpable and the super real. Therefore, his poetry abounds with winged creatures, heavenly bodies, and plants and animals endowed with special powers. For example, the first two poems in this anthology, "Doubting Icarus" and "I Know There's Someone Dwelling within Me" (both from *The Dark Stamp of God*), feature winged creatures and flight. "Doubting Icarus" rewrites the Icarus myth in order to reconsider untapped or undiscovered potential. Perhaps Icarus's demise is not so much a cautionary tale of hubris, but addresses the struggle to realize human potential fully, perhaps for the poet to realize their gifts fully.

Yet these mythological creatures also point to the limits of mythology to create or sustain meaning. For example, "I Know There's Someone Dwelling within Me" features a winged creature—perhaps an angel—capable of stimulating an essential yet unknowable part of the speaker's soul. The creature, akin to a "sleepwalking angel," wanders down the lonely corridors of the speaker's psyche, "Uselessly plucking the sweetest strings / of my heart." And yet this unknown "guest" may be a gift from the divine, a cosmic nudge toward self-discovery, and thus perhaps a return to a prefallen state. Sarabia sees here an emblematic split within the speaker as they search for the divinity within, but unable to identify it, remains lost and permanently fallen. Underscoring the dilemma, the creature's music alludes to the primordial harmony before the separation, now a sonic reminder of what has been lost.[19]

In a strikingly different vein, "The Archangel" (from *Sacrificials*) takes up the Judeo-Christian theme of fall and redemption in order to contemplate the dependent nature of good and evil. The speaker is the proud owner of an odd sculpture of an archangel that originally stood over a vanquished Satan. Yet the speaker has had the "Tempter" removed, and all that remains is the solitary angel; "its vibrant / colors have darkened."

Perhaps in its own fallen state, the angel engages the speaker in a conversation about good and evil:

> Do you know what ontological condition is worse than that of an angel?
> It didn't occur to me, I responded puzzled
> An angel who has been separated from his demon
> Didn't you know that it was evil's awful wings that sustained my pure flight?

Ultimately, the archangel can know himself as such—an agent of good, a representative of god—only in the presence of evil, his supposed opposite. Without Satan, the angel has no meaning or purpose and thus is doomed to fade, then disappear: "Any day now I will enter the studio and only see on the wall / the washed-out stroke of a sunbeam." As the poem itself yields to vacancy and silence, the absence of evil signifies the collapse of meaning. Although Judeo-Christian mythology promises the ultimate triumph of good over evil for the faithful—meaning fully realized—Bustos's poem suggests that such an outcome would be meaningless, an encounter with the existential void that might seem more like hell than heaven.

This move to invert the meaning of received mythology marks much of Bustos's poetic encounter with the fantastic. Returning to "Jonah's Monologue," the erasure of divisions or boundaries, noted earlier, results in a jarring rewriting of the myth. God, as delivered by the Hebrew Bible, is nowhere to be found, and thus Jonah does not struggle to understand his obligations to god but must consider his relationship with an immense animal with godlike omnipresence. If there still is a god left in the myth, it is the unknowable natural world, enveloping humankind and thus demanding a reckoning, an attempt to understand that which may well surpass understanding.

Finally, we might consider an additional example of Bustos's use of mythology in order to consider the absence or death of god. If "Jonah's Monologue" offers a radical displacement of god, then "Scene at Marbella" (from *The Season of Thirst*) presents his death. The god of Genesis who first "rolled over the waters" is now a drowned chimera, a mythic monster of disparate parts, not unlike the Judeo-Christian tradition itself, made up of ancient and disparate Middle Eastern folktales. Here the beast lies inert and inscrutable as onlookers try to make sense of the scene. Furthermore, where the tradition stresses the eating of god's flesh as the sacred act of redemption, here onlookers "ask themselves," according to Sarabia's reading, "if they do not run the risk of poisoning themselves with food that no longer provides any sustenance."[20]

In a larger sense, Bustos's address of modern existential doubt thoroughly undermines Judeo-Christian-based epistemology, entertaining the possibility or even likelihood that there is no god, at least not the one found in Judeo-Christian mythology. The modern existential state requires the individual (and the group) to create meaning elsewhere; and though this state comes with great doubt, even despair, in Bustos's cosmos, wonder and despair may coexist.

And so, we return to the question of Bustos's metaphysics and its relation to Blackness. Though, to this point, we have addressed the content of Bustos's metaphysics, the answer may lie in its location, more specifically in Caribbean and Afro-Colombian culture, particularly that of the northern coast and the specific spaces in which that culture unfolds. For Bustos, the connection between the "Caribbean imaginary"[21] and Blackness consists of music, dance, and the larger mythic fields that they invoke. He argues that the rhythms and rituals of everyday life for Blacks in Cartagena find their way into many poems; music, dance, food, dress, and so on signal viable responses to this existential challenge. For Bustos, "dance is essentially the site of myth, the location where being resides, the instant when being returns to the center."[22] Or, as we mentioned earlier, modern poetry's dilemma, for Bustos, is over the potency or impotence of the mythopoetic; meaning and meaninglessness are the "two faces on the coin we call poetry."[23] Thus, the myth and ritual inherent in Black music and dance, their ability to invoke the divine or to access the super real, may provide, in one sense, a robust response to the challenge of existential freedom. At moments, Bustos asserts that in "ancestral poetry, the word is full of potential. The world is the word that founds it; what's more, here poetry subsumes the word; it is also the gesture, dance, song, and ritual."[24] If at least momentarily music, dance, and their concomitant rituals provide the salvific mythology to fill the void, to heal the primordial wound, then the Caribbean and Afro-Colombian Blackness lie at the very center of Bustos's metaphysics. Not only are they necessary for his poetic imaginings, they may serve as a cogent response to the crisis.

In this sense, "A Man with Black Skin" (also from *The Dark Stamp of God*) presents Blackness not so much as a stand-in for oppression but as reference to the cosmos, his dance as his means of experiencing the universal or the divine: "Deep within the dance / His vast heaven spins on." Likewise, the Black women of "Palenqueras" (also from *The Dark Stamp of God*), unschooled and speaking an allegedly corrupted form of Spanish, nevertheless perform work that provides insight into essences. That they carry large bowls of fruit on their heads to sell in the streets, "their heads know / the exact weight of the world." Or in "Orishas" (from *The Season of Thirst*), a girl dancing is able to conjure the gods of Lucumí (or what outsiders would call Santería): "beautiful warriors with flutes, ancient divinities / gaze at her / The girl seems to recognize them." Through dance created by her Black community, she is able to access the divine. In all three poems, Bustos presents Black rituals as sites and occasions for metaphysical reflection.

Yet, Bustos's immersion in Blackness goes well beyond the poems that make obvious references. In our reading, Bustos invokes Colombia's northern coast and the Caribbean more generally as Black spaces—defined by its people, their speech, rituals, and cultural forms—capable of reflections on being, nothingness, and freedom. For example, "Chronicle of the Courtyard," whose sacred space, as we have seen, may hint at the divine, makes no explicit reference to Blackness, yet the setting and women derive from Bustos's childhood Caribbean milieu. The work and ritual of shelling rice help to define this community of Caribbean women and serve here to connect the women and the courtyard to the natural world. The women and the moon complement one another in the ongoing transformation of the natural world. According to this reading, the space of the dance in "Orishas" and the courtyard in "Chronicle of the Courtyard" provide the communal site for rituals that in turn define the community and create meaning through gestures toward the universe or the divine.

Furthermore, that an Afro-Colombian chooses to write in an existential/metaphysical vein is of enormous importance. Traditionally, we understand the conceptual space of philosophy as a nominally white one. We accept, uncritically, the continental and US pragmatist philosophical traditions as defined, dominated, and owned by white men—with the outlying exceptions, more often than not, proving the rule. That Bustos lays claim to this alleged white space and makes it his own asserts the power of the Black artist to access and reshape whichever artistic/philosophical tradition she, he, or they see fit. In this sense, Bustos unapologetically asserts himself as central to the occidental tradition and world of ideas. And as he works to revise Greco-Roman and Judeo-Christian mythology, either to expose their impotence in a modern world or to reassign them meaning to save them from irrelevance, Bustos accrues to himself an authority to interpret and revise, an authority seldom recognized in the Black writer.

Like so many Caribbean writers, Bustos transforms the occidental tradition by placing the Caribbean at its center and using it as the lens through which the "relationship between notions of human freedom and notions of human essence," as Fred Moten puts it, can best be explored.[25] In other words, Bustos invokes a Black radical imaginary as the crux of his metaphysics. Just as Toni Morrison reimagines the American literary canon as a meditation on Blackness (and whiteness);[26] just as Paul Gilroy rethinks modernity, the Enlightenment, reason, and freedom with slave trading and slavery as their foundation;[27] just as Nikole Hannah-Jones and others reconceive American history with enslaved Blacks and their descendants as its very engine;[28] just as Manuel Zapata Olivella rewrites the history of the Western Hemisphere from a Black perspective;[29] or just as Derek Walcott presents the Caribbean as the backdrop for an epic struggle for survival and meaning,[30] Bustos invokes the Caribbean as a site of contemporary existential thought and poetics.

Such a focus finds its justification in the long and brutal history of European contact with the Caribbean. As the original site of Western conquest and colonialism, the African slave trade, and plantation slavery, the Caribbean served as the crucible in which Europeans, indigenous communities, Africans, and their descendants struggled over the very nature of being, freedom, personhood, and the possibilities of popular government. Over and against the subjugation of Native Americans and Africans, the Dutch, French, Spanish, and British began to sharpen their understanding of sovereignty and individual liberty. And as Orlando Patterson points out, the embodied antithesis of freedom, the enslaved, fought to the death to make real the ideals their European tormentors attempted to reserve for themselves.[31] The Haitian Revolution—the first revolt of the enslaved to result in the creation of a sovereign Black republic—was fought to realize for Haitians the ideals of the French Revolution: liberty, fraternity, equality. An independent Haiti went on to provide vital support to Simón Bolívar and his campaigns to free Gran Colombia from Spanish colonial rule, support predicated on the abolition of slavery. Indeed, the Haitians' defeat of the British,

French, and Spanish, and their strident defense of Enlightenment principles, reverberated across the white Western world, as it was forced to contemplate Blacks and Blackness, not simply as antitheses to freedom but as constitutive elements of modernity.

As such, Bustos's Caribbean serves as a fertile site for the exploration of freedom and the nature of being. Here, freedom expands well beyond the immediately political (freedom from tyranny, freedom to vote, assemble peacefully, worship, speak freely, etc.) to the philosophical and metaphysical where being, meaning, and humankind's relation to the cosmos take center stage. In its Caribbean context, the enduring ambivalence, the both/and animating Bustos's poetry finds its fullest expression, where humankind confronts the terror and delight in the eternal struggle to create meaning anew. Indeed, meaning may finally reside not on one side or the other of the wonder/doubt axis but in the very nature of the opposition itself.

By way of illustration, we might think of "Pendulum" (from *The Incessant Pupil*) as an ars poetica of sorts, though Bustos himself has never made this claim, that asserts his poetics, in a Caribbean context, as the stage on which we all might explore the threat and possibility of freedom.

Pendulum

The pendulum
Does nothing else but look for its center

It's strange to see it going hypnotically
from one extreme to the other

It searches for stillness
For this it moves

It looks for itself
That's why it doesn't find itself

for Alberto Abello

Just as the pendulum moves from one periphery through the center to the other extreme, using motion to find stasis, the poem employs sound (here language) to contemplate silence. Neither the pendulum nor the poem, as far as Bustos is concerned, can reach its destination or find an enduring truth without an encounter with its opposite. In a sense, periphery and center, motion and stasis, good and evil, life and death, god and man are at least symbiotic, the one dependent on the other for its existence and meaning. A step further would suggest that the opposites ultimately conflate, or at least the border dividing inside and outside, center and periphery, sound and silence, tends to disappear, leaving the motion of the pendulum, the process of conflation as the thing itself. The very action of the pendulum and the poem signals the role, function, or even "meaning" of poetry in the twenty-first century. Here, the poem serves as a staging of sorts, creating "the conditions to make possible the metaphoric formulation and interpretation of reality."[32]

Put another way, this play between seeming opposites serves as a surrender, giving oneself fully to the freedom and crisis that the wound and its proliferating implications offer; in this sense, the poem does not mean but *is*.[33] Or as Santos puts it, "[T]he imagination and the imaginary exist as means and ends unto themselves."[34] Fully alive to the existential challenge of its moment, Bustos's poetry wields the Black radical imaginary tradition to confront the existential burden of freedom. Ultimately, he offers a Caribbean universe as a means by which humankind may face the failure of mythology, the void of language, the foreclosure of history, the death of the divine . . . and possibly find meaning there.

SEMANTICS

of the WORLD

El oscuro sello de Dios

The Dark Stamp of God

1988

Ícaro dudoso

Tal vez
llevamos alas a la espalda
Y no sabemos

Doubting Icarus

Maybe
we have wings on our backs
And we don't even know

Hay alguien que yo sé morándome

Hay alguien que yo sé morándome
Arrastra sus alas de ángel sonámbulo
como quien busca una puerta
               entre largos corredores
Triste de sí
Pulsando inútil las cuerdas más dulces
               de mi alma

Quizás me existiera desde siempre
¿De qué ancho cielo habrá venido
               este huésped que no conozco?

a J. Arleis

I Know There's Someone Dwelling within Me

I know there's someone dwelling within me
He drags his wings like a sleepwalking angel
like a lonely soul looking for a door
                    along the long corridors
So sad
Uselessly plucking the sweetest strings
                    of my heart

Maybe he has always been here
From what wide heaven has come
              this guest I do not know?

      for J. Arleis

Cada día volvemos a inventar el paraíso

Cada día volvemos a inventar el paraíso
Cada día la espada fogosa del ángel
calcinándonos el alma
Cada día
alejamos nuestros pasos
sin saber ni siquiera qué es
                lo que se nos niega

Every Day We Remake Paradise

Every day we remake paradise
Every day the angel's ardent sword
scorches our hearts
Every day
we walk away
without even knowing what
                we've lost

Odiseo

La guerra que descaminó mis días
también me ha entregado su rosa
Cada cual ha de ir en busca de su rosa
Una rosa violenta
Sé que hay una
para cada hombre en la guerra
Al final serás una sombra, un ánfora
vacía. Pero habrás oído cantar
                a las sirenas

a Raymundo Gómez-Cásseres

Odysseus

The war that threw my life off course
has also given me its compass rose[1]
Each must go in search of their compass
A violent rose
I know that there's one
for every man in the war
Finally, you'll be a shadow, an empty Amphora.[2]
But you'll have heard
        the sirens' song

for Raymundo Gómez-Cásseres

Ajedrez

Alguien ha dejado abandonado este juego
Aquí las fichas en desorden. El caballo
      inicia un eterno salto en el aire
La torre—menudos peones y guerreros
caídos—como si hubiera sido tomada
           por asalto
El paseo desolado de la reina que a veces
asoma su pálido rostro entre las almenas
y parece aún no entender lo que ha pasado

Chess Set

Someone has abandoned this game
Here the pieces are strewn about. The horse
      begins its eternal jump into the air
The tower—little peons and fallen
warriors—as if taken
                      by storm
The queen on her desolate walk sometimes
shows her pale face between the battlements
and looks as if she still doesn't understand

Jungla

La jungla no está solo
en el corazón del tigre o en su garra
El sigilo del aire, el rugido, el oscuro
horror, la dentellada
cuelgan al lado izquierdo de tu pecho
          como inocente medalla
Un día cualquiera
te asomarás al espejo
y pudieras ser la primera víctima

Jungle

The jungle doesn't reside only
in the tiger's heart, or in his claws
The menace of the air, the roar, the dark
horror, the bite
these hang on the left side of your chest
          like an innocent medallion
Any day
you pick up the mirror
you could be the first victim

Socrática

No confíes en la respuesta del espejo
que tu cuerpo interroga
Lo que somos o no somos
es el secreto que hubiera salvado
del suicidio a la esfinge tebana
La verdad no es negocio de hombres
Recuérdalo
Siempre serás tu más íntimo forastero

Socratic

Don't trust the mirror's reflection
which interrogates your body
That which we are or are not
is the secret that might have saved
the Theban Sphinx[3] from suicide
Truth is not the business of men
Remember this
You will always be your most intimate stranger

Palenqueras

Mujeres grandes que llevan
tesoros blancos en los dientes
Sentadas parloteando en lengua extraña
como enormes diosas ya olvidadas
Acaso mejor que el sabio
conozcan sus cabezas
el peso exacto de las cosas del mundo

    a Amelia

Palenqueras[4]

Big women who carry
white treasures in their teeth
Seated chatting in strange tongues
like enormous goddesses, already forgotten
Perhaps better than the wise man
their heads know
the exact weight of the world

   for Amelia

Monólogo del verdugo

Cuando el rey baja la mano
debo entender que hay que aniquilar a la víctima
Si la deja a media asta
se trata entonces de una mutilación simple
Si un poco más abajo de una mutilación doble
Ignoro si alguna vez ha levantado la mano
                           absolutorio
Diarias son las inmolaciones. Los días
no son menos violentos que las noches
¿Llegará un descanso para mi fatigado brazo?
En verdad no soy mejor ni peor
                que el resto de los mortales

Hangman's Monologue

When the king lowers his hand
I must execute the victim
If he raises his hand only halfway
I cut off a limb
A little lower, two limbs
I don't know if he has ever
         pardoned anyone
The sacrifices are daily. The days
are no less violent than the nights
Will there be any rest for my weary arm?
Honestly, I'm no better or worse
         than the rest of the mortals

Un hombre de piel negra

Un hombre de piel negra danza
con un pie en el corazón
        y el otro más allá
en el asiento espesísimo del alma
Acampado en el baile
Hila su vasto cielo

A Man with Black Skin

A man with black skin dances
With a foot in his heart
        and the other far off
in the teeming seat of the soul
Deep within the dance
His vast heaven spins on

En el traspatio del cielo

On the Back Porch of Heaven

1993

Árbol camajorú

I

En lo hondo del traspatio
más allá del mango, de los durmientes ciruelos
está el árbol solo, el solitario camajorú
rodeado de sed, hechizado en el tajo de luz
en que una vez se le abrió el cielo
Todos lo miramos de lejos
Pero sus ramas ya no podemos verlas. Sus ramas
                            son invisibles
Sus ramas volaron a lo alto. Sus ramas quedaron
                            prendidas en lo alto
Y son ahora el techo del mundo

II

Bajo las raíces del árbol camajorú hay otro árbol
El camajorú de la tierra. El camajorú del cielo
Al camajorú de la tierra se asciende bajando
como en la escalera de un sueño
Y echa un fruto redondo como preñez de luna
Del camajorú del cielo poco sabemos
Dicen que si uno come su fruto puede quedar ciego
Los ángeles de él se alimentan

a Pedro Badrán

Camajorú Tree[1]

I

Way back in the backyard
past the mango, past the sleeping plum
there is a lone tree, the solitary camajorú
surrounded by thirst,
once the heavens opened up
in a beam of light and held the tree transfixed
We look at it from afar
But we can no longer see its branches.
      They're invisible
They flew high. And there they remained
      held way up above us
And they are now the roof of the world

II

Below the roots of the camajorú tree there is another tree
The camajorú of the earth. The camajorú of heaven
You climb the camajorú of the earth by going down
like the steps in a dream
And it produces a fruit round like a pregnant moon
We know little about the camajorú of heaven
They say that if one eats the fruit one could go blind
The angels feed on it

 for Pedro Badrán

La visita

"dame un poco de ese dulce de tamarindo"

Dijo el ángel
que en lugar de voz sonaba un prodigioso metal
                                      en la garganta

El ángel estaba asomado a la ventana
bajo la enredadera llamada trompeta de ángeles
Pero él no tocaba sus trompetas sino que repetía
"dame un poco de ese dulce de tamarindo"
En su camisón blanquísimo se veían manchas
                                        desleídas
Una nube azul cubría sus ojos abiertos
como alguien detenido en perpetuo asombro
"es que me manché el vestido comiendo pepas
                                        de camajorú"
Dijeron las sonajas que agitaba en su garganta
Y yo le contesté
"lávalas con agua de astromelias
para que cuando regreses no te regañe tu madre"

Afuera parecía que hubiera caído a la tierra
el más suntuoso de los astros

    a Gustavo Adolfo

The Visit

"give me a taste of that *dulce de tamarindo*"[2]

The angel said
but instead of his voice an incredible metallic noise rattled
                                        in his throat

The angel appeared in the window
below the creeping vines called the "trumpet of angels"
But he didn't play his trumpet, he just repeated
"Give me a taste of that dulce de tamarindo"
There were many faint stains on his pure white
                                        nightshirt
A blue cloud covered his opened eyes
like someone frozen in perpetual amazement
"I stained my shirt while eating fruit
                                  from the camajorú"
He said with a rattle in his throat
And I answered him
"wash it with water of *astromelias*[3]
so that when you return you won't be scolded by your mother"

Outside it looked as though there had fallen to the ground
the most magnificent asteroids

    for Gustavo Adolfo

Al otro lado del mundo

Al otro lado del mundo rondaba el mar
la voz salitrosa del agua, su bronco rumor
su desnudez muy blanca en la punta del día
Un animal de agua moraba más allá del mundo
Y detrás de su voz estaba el silencio
el profundo respiro de algún ser acechante
Pero yo no lo veía. Yo lo soñaba por los ojos
                de la madre
cuando en las tardes rallaba con sus manos
                        una luna
que ya diluida parecía
      la leche purísima del coco

   a Amaury de Dios

On the Other Side of the World

On the other side of the world, the sea hovered
the salty voice of the water, its rough murmur,
its very white nudity at high noon
An animal of the water dwelled beyond the world
And behind the voice was the silence
the deep breath of some lurking being
But I didn't see him. I dreamed him through the eyes
                               of the mother
when in the afternoon she would scratch a moon
                                        with her hands
when diluted looked like
            pure coconut milk

    for Amaury de Dios

Matarratón

El árbol de los relinchos lo llamamos
Basta tocarlo con la mano y el árbol
                se llena de relinchos
Entonces nos ponemos bajo las ramas
                y soñamos un caballo

Y este es el conjuro del caballo

ángel frondoso que estás en el árbol
venga a nosotros el más fino caballo
las firmes patas del caballo
la grupa sudorosa del caballo
el viento impetuoso del caballo
las alas invisibles del caballo
la blanca maravilla del caballo

Y el ángel que habitaba en el árbol
                nos lo daba

Matarratón[4]

We call it the tree of the horses' neighs
Just touch it with your hand and the tree
                is filled with neighs
So, we stand below the branches
                  and dream a horse

And this is the horse's spell

feathered angel that's in the tree
send us the most exquisite horse
the horse's hard hooves
the horse's sweaty haunches
the horse's impetuous wind
the horse's invisible wings
the horse's magnificent white

And the angel that lived in the tree
                            gave him to us

Crónica de la madre

Dios creó las seis de la mañana para que la madre
                                         despierte
Y nosotros podamos recoger los mangos
                        caídos durante la noche
cuando el aire es todavía un secreto
                    dicho en voz muy baja por la sombra

Ramiro encuentra los más grandes y los muestra
Pequeños trofeos recogidos en la más dulce guerra
                             entre los hermanos

La madre atiza el día y suelta los olores

Sobre las cuatro patas de la mesa como un animal manso
las hojas del bijao abren su fruta humeante

Desayuna el mundo

    a Enrique

The Mother's Chronicle

God created six o'clock in the morning for the mother
                                        to wake up
And so that we can gather the mangos
                          that fell during the night
when the air is still a secret
            said in a very low voice by the shadows

Ramiro finds the largest ones and shows them
Little trophies collected in the sweetest war
                        between brothers

The mother stirs up the day and releases its scent.

On the table's four legs like a docile animal
the leaves of the *bijao* tree[5] open offering their steaming fruit

The world eats its breakfast

    for Enrique

Crónica del mediodía

La luz se empoza en los techos de zinc
Un pájaro canta
Y su voz es un hilo tendido entre el pico
y el color amarillo que ha hecho nido
                    en lo alto
Sería dichosa la madre
si sobre él pudiera tender la ropa recién lavada

Cuando el pájaro acabe de cantar
podría venirse abajo el cielo

Midday Chronicle

Light pools on the tin roofs
A bird sings
And his voice is a thread hung from his beak
and the yellow that has made his nest
                        on high
The mother would be happy
if she could put freshly washed clothes on it

When the bird stops singing
heaven could fall

Crónica de la hermana mayor

Dios creó las cuatro de la tarde
para que los árboles hablen con la brisa
Para que la hermana mayor regrese
y yo pueda esperarla junto a la verja

La hermana mayor con sus dos largas trenzas

En la esquina
la acacia ha encendido cada una de sus flores
y parece un fino candelabro a plena luz

Las columnas del parque como las patas
                    de seis garzas blancas

El ángel siempre atareado mirando bajo el ala
                              de las cosas
me murmura al oído lo que dicen los árboles
"son las cuatro la hermana vuelve"

The Big Sister's Chronicle

God created four o'clock in the afternoon
so that the trees can talk to the breeze
So that the big sister can return
and so that I can wait for her, leaning against the fence

The big sister with her two long braids

At the corner
the *acacia*[6] has lit every one of its flowers
it looks like a magnificent candelabra full of light

The columns in the park like the legs
                    of six white herons

The ever-busy angel looking under the wings
                                of things
murmurs in my ear what the trees say
"it's four o'clock your sister's coming back"

Crónica de la noche

"es un ave muy negra arrastrando las grandes alas"

Anuncia la hermana mientras suelta las oscuras
                                        trenzas
mirando más allá de la ventana, entre los árboles

Y yo adivino la noche deslizándose
como si hubiera estado todo el tiempo oculta
                           bajo el palo de tamarindo

La sombra del ciruelo, la sombra de la casa,
                         la sombra del mecedor

Todo el día
la sombra ha seguido las cosas como animal manso
                         con bozales de luz

Ahora un aliento desconocido la esparce
Algo nace de la espalda de las cosas y las envuelve
y late y trepa invisible
Algo se duerme en el plumaje de los árboles

Pero todo empieza junto al palo de tamarindo
Algo de la frescura de la noche queda siempre
escondido entre sus ramas, bajo su fresco sombrero

"es un pavorreal"

añade la hermana, mirando las estrellas
peinando largamente la noche

    a Nubia

Night's Chronicle

"it's a very black bird dragging its big wings"

The sister announces as she lets go of her dark
                                                        braids
looking beyond the window, between the trees

And I feel the night sneaking up
as if it had always been hiding
                            under the tamarind tree

The plum tree's shade, the house's shadow
                            the shadow of the rocking chair

All day
the shadow has followed these things like a tamed animal
                            with a muzzle of light

Now an unknown breath spreads it
Something is born from the back of things and envelops them
and beats and climbs invisible
Something goes to sleep in the plumage of the trees

But all begins together at the trunk of the tamarind tree
Something from the crispness of the night always remains
hidden between its branches, below its cool hat

"it's a peacock"

the sister adds looking at the stars
slowly combing the night

    for Nubia

Crónica del patio

Descuidadas mujeres han regado
todo el arroz pilado durante el día
y el patio es un fantasma silencioso
La luna se ha derramado gota a gota
Sin embargo
su delgado cuenco sigue intacto allá arriba
Las piedras, la palma, el cercado de palos . . .
que ahora no son verdes ni malvas ni dorados
como si entre la luz y la sombra
volvieran las cosas—extrañas—a su condición
                        más verdadera

Chronicle of the Courtyard

Careless women have spilled
all the rice shelled during the day
and the courtyard is a silent ghost
The moon has spilled out drop by drop
Nevertheless
its little hollow remains intact there above
The rocks, the palm, the fence of sticks . . .
that now are not green nor mauve nor golden
as if between the light and the shadow
things returned—rarified—to their
                    truest state

Vuelo y construcción del caballo de palo

Del matarratón más puro lo cortarás
de un palo llovido por las lluvias de mayo
de la vara más alta
para que ya esté acostumbrado al cielo

A la mitad del día lo cortarás
con el agudo canto de tres grillos labrarás
                              sus ancas
y en sus patas traseras soplarás
                              el soplo de la sábila

Cuida que no esté cerca una mujer muy vieja
                        mirándote de espaldas
pues su mirada podría enfermar su vuelo

Sobre el techo de tu casa lo dejarás tres días

Entonces sujétalo
pero no con la mano sino con el aire de la mano
como si tu mano estuviera soñando
Ahora
sólo ten cuidado de no tropezar con las nubes
o el asombro callado de los pájaros

    a Fernando Linero

Flight and Construction of the Hobby Horse

From the purest *matarratón* tree you will cut it
from a stem watered by May's rains
from a branch so high
that it's already at home in heaven

In the middle of the day you will cut it
with the piercing song of three crickets, you will carve
                                    its haunches
and on its hind legs you will blow
                        the puff of the aloe vera

Take care that a very old woman isn't near
                        looking at you from behind
because her look could ruin its flight

You will leave it on your roof for three days

So hold it
not with your hand but with the air of your hand
as if your hand were dreaming
Now
only take care not to trip over the clouds
or the birds' amazed silence

    for Fernando Linero

Crónica del árbol de agua

Un día
Dios sembró un árbol de agua
para que lloviera

Y vio Dios que era buena la tierra del cielo
para sembrar la lluvia

Y hubo así estaciones

Y cada cierto tiempo
el viento que agitan las alas de mil ángeles
estremece el árbol y sus hojas se esparcen
                                    sobre la tierra

Entonces comienza el invierno
Y nosotros ponemos ollas y cántaros para recoger
                                    la lluvia

Chronicle of the Tree of Water

One day
God planted the tree of water
so that it would rain

And God saw the soil of heaven was good
for sowing rain

And so there were seasons

And every so often
the wind from the rustle of the wings of a thousand angels
        makes the tree shake and its leaves to scatter
                over the land

So winter begins
And we put out pots and jugs to collect
        the rain

Poema de las pertenencias

A la hermana pertenecía el lado izquierdo
                de la casa
Y las piedras pulidas que parecen soles
También eran suyos el color amarillo
y la palabra "alamud" pronunciada suavemente,
los botones en forma de pequeños emperadores,
el santo y seña para entrar y salir de los espejos
(una vez quedó aprisionada en el espejo de la sala
y debió revelarme su secreto)
Eran míos
el fulgor de las nubes que anuncian la lluvia,
el juego de la peregrina, el palo yaya, las telas
crujientes como las alas de las grandes moscas,
la mitad de la palabra para abrir el día...
La otra mitad era de la hermana
Subíamos a la ventana bajo los trompeteros
y repetíamos: "sayana," "sayana"
y la luz se asomaba como doblando una esquina
                del mundo
A veces no despertábamos y desde el sueño
         soñábamos sayana

Era entonces más brillante el cielo

Nunca nos preguntamos
a quién pertenecían los dados cargados
                del tiempo

Poem of Belongings

The sister owned the left side
                           of the house
And the polished stones that look like suns
Hers too were the color yellow
and the word "alamud,"[7] pronounced gently,
the buttons in the form of little emperors,
the password to enter and exit the mirrors
(one time she was trapped in the living room mirror
and she had to reveal her secret to me)
Mine were
the brilliance of the clouds that announced the rain,
the game of hopscotch, the yaya stick,[8] the brittle
fabrics like the wings of the big flies,
half of the word to open the day . . .
The other half was the sister's
We climbed to the window below the *trompeteros*[9]
and we repeated "sayana," "sayana"[10]
and the light appeared as it turned a corner
                           of the world
Sometimes we wouldn't wake up and from the dream
                           we dream of sayana

The heavens were brighter then

We never asked ourselves
who owned time's
                           loaded dice

Poema a la hermana menor

El cielo estaba a tiro de guijarros
en aquellos días, ¿recuerdas?

Bastaba trazar en surco las alas, los cajones
saltar con cuidado
como subiendo en un solo pie una escalera empinada
cuyo extremo se recostaba en el sueño

El aire se atareaba
de nubes bajas y verdes en aquel juego, ¿recuerdas?
Jaime, Hugo, Deya, Alberto, Gonzalo, Anamaría...
¿En qué momento equivocamos el pie
y tropezamos contra los astros ingenuos
que iluminaban aquel juego? Y luego
como si un ser malvado hubiera borrado los surcos
                                        con una rama
sólo han quedado confusos trazos sobre la tierra
las débiles líneas, los fallidos guijarros del poema

Yo tenía muy buen tino, ¿recuerdas?

Poem for the Little Sister

The heavens were just a stone's throw away
in those days, do you remember?

All we had to do was draw the squares and the wings in a line
jump carefully
as if climbing by foot a steep stair
whose end lay in a dream

The air was busy
with clouds, low and green, in that game, do you remember?
Jaime, Hugo, Deya, Alberto, Gonzalo, Anamaría . . .
When did we lose our way
and trip on the naïve stars
that lit the game? And later
it was as if a demon had swept the lines away
                              with a branch
but still there were faint strokes on the ground
the faded lines, the failed pebbles of the poem

And I had good aim, do you remember?

Balada de la casa

Hallarás una casa con un nombre extraño
      que intentarás pronunciar en vano
Y muros del color de los buenos sueños
Pero tú no verás ese color
Tampoco beberás el vino rojo de los ciruelos
            que ensancha los recuerdos
En la verja
un niño con un libro entreabierto
Pregúntale por el camino de los grandes árboles
cuyos frutos guarda un animal
que adormece a los andantes con sólo mirarlos
Y él contestará mientras conversa
          con un ángel de alas verdes
(como si fuera otro niño que juega al ángel
y se hubiera colocado anchas hojas de plátano a la espalda)
moviendo apenas los labios en un leve conjuro
"el canto del gallo no es azul sino de un rosa dormido
como el primer claro del día"
Y tú no entenderás. Y sin embargo
hallarás un zaguán que yo recorrí inmenso
donde cuelga el retrato de un señor que resplandece
         levemente, con el corazón en la mano
Y al fondo, muy al fondo
el alma de la casa sentada en una mecedora, cantando
Pero tú no la escucharás
Pues, en ese instante
un sonido lejano ajará el horizonte
Y el niño habrá pasado la última de las páginas

Ballad of the House

You will find a house with a strange name
       that you will try to pronounce in vain
And walls the color of good dreams
But you won't see the color
Nor will you drink the plums' red wine
                 that fills your memories
At the gate
a boy with a half-opened book
Ask him for the road with the big trees
whose fruit is guarded by an animal
who puts walkers to sleep just by looking at them
And he will answer while talking
                   with an angel with green wings
(as if it were another boy who plays at being an angel
and would put the wide plantain leaves on his back)
barely moving his lips in a little spell
"the cock's crow is not blue but a sleeping pink
like the first light of day"
And you won't understand. Nevertheless
you will find a long hallway that I walked
where the portrait of a gentleman hangs; he glows
            faintly, with his heart in his hand
And at the end, the far end
the house's soul is seated in a rocking chair, singing
But you won't hear it
Because, at this moment
a distant sound will come from the horizon
And the boy will have turned the last page

Palenquera

Abre la boca ancha
y su pregón llena la calle

Los niños miran los pies descalzos
                    sobre la tierra
buscando las raíces de este árbol
en cuya copa maduran todos los frutos

Palenquera

She opens her wide mouth
and her cry fills the street

The children look at their bare feet
                             on the ground
looking for the roots of the tree
in whose cup all the fruits ripen

La estación de la sed

The Season of Thirst

1998

Crónica

A los pocos días de nacido apareció el demonio
Se posó sobre el cabezal de la cama
siguiendo con su pico el movimiento de mis ojos
Una vez más
madre lo espanta con un grito en medio
                         del recuerdo
y agrega sonreída:
"ahora estarías ciego, hijo mío"
"sí, madre"—digo
mirando fijamente el vacío horizonte

Chronicle

Just a few days after I was born the devil appeared
He passed over the bed's headboard
following the movement of my eyes with his beak
Once again
mother scares him with a cry in the middle
                          of a memory
then adds with a smile:
"now you would be blind, my son"
"yes, mother"—I say
staring at the empty horizon

Cotidiano

Como sucede con los cuadros que cuelgan
                         en las paredes
cada mañana sorprendes
una leve inclinación de tu adentro
Cada mañana crees corregir este desnivel
Pero entre la primera posición y la segunda
queda siempre un residuo
una brizna de polvo que se acumula

Sobre esta oscura aritmética se edifica tu alma

Everyday

It happens with the paintings that hang
                         on the walls
every morning you're surprised to find them
at a slight angle
Every morning you think to correct this irregularity
But between the first position and the second
there's always a shadow
a trace of the dust that accumulates

Your soul is made of this curious arithmetic

Ciempiés

El ciempiés en el piso del retrete
tratando de escalar la pared
O braceando
en la pequeña vorágine de la taza

Las lisas, inexpugnables paredes
Las cien patas de tu alma

Centipede

The centipede on the bathroom floor
trying to climb the wall
Or flailing
in the little vortex of the sink

The smooth, unassailable walls
Your soul's one hundred feet

El pajarero

A este hombre lo vi niño
llevando en sus manos una jaula
Un poco más usado el gesto de ociosa
                                   inocencia
la sigue llevando como quien porta una luz
o un distraído sueño
El pájaro ya no está
En verdad nunca ha estado
Pero, a veces, se detiene y aguza al aire el oído
como si escuchara su canto

The Bird Catcher

I saw this man as a boy
carrying a birdcage in his hands
A slightly more worn gesture of idle
                      innocence
he continued to carry it like someone carrying a light
or a daydream
The bird is no longer there
In truth, it had never been there
But, sometimes, he stops and pricks up his ears
as if he's heard its song

Una vez en un sitio

Una vez en un sitio
vi un muchacho que bailaba
        con los ojos cerrados
casi no tocaba los pies con la tierra
Su piel era oscura y hermosa
sin mácula alguna
Entonces me dije:
¿Cuánto durará su danza?

a Pedro Blas

One Time at the Spot

One time at the spot
I saw this guy dancing
        with his eyes closed
his feet barely touched the ground
His skin was dark and beautiful
without a single mark
So I said to myself:
How long will his dance last?

    for Pedro Blas

Botánica

La hoja ama la luz
Pero la raíz es negocio de sombras
Sobre este asunto capital
el árbol no puede andarse
        por las ramas

Botánica[1]

The leaf loves the light
But the root is the business of shadows
On this key point
the tree cannot
        beat around the bush

Cuento

Aves perversas
han comido todas las marcas, las migajas
                    protectoras
Hansel y Grethel
están ahora solos en el terrorífico bosque

Story

Wicked birds
have eaten all the signs, the protective
                              breadcrumbs
Hansel and Gretel
are now alone in the terrifying forest

El don

A un hombre que cae le es dado por un instante
el don del colibrí
Detenido en el aire descubre que siempre
en cualquier posición en la que esté, estará cayendo
Entonces le devuelve las alas al colibrí
y empieza a caminar sobre la línea del horizonte

The Gift

A man who falls is given for an instant
the hummingbird's gift
Suspended in the air he discovers that
in whatever position he might be, he will always be falling
Then he returns the wings to the hummingbird
and starts to walk on the line of the horizon

Escena de Marbella

Junto a las piedras está Dios bocarriba
Los pescadores en fila tiraron largamente de la red
Y ahora yace allí con sus ojos blancos mirando al cielo
Parece un bañista definitivamente distraído
Parece un gran pez gordo de cola muy grande
Pero es solo Dios
hinchado y con escamas impuras
¿Cuánto tiempo habrá rodado sobre las aguas?
Los curiosos observan la pesca monstruosa
Algunos separan una porción y la llevan
                                      para sus casas
Otros se preguntan si será conveniente
comer de un alimento que ha estado tanto tiempo
                        expuesto a la intemperie

a Juan Marchena, cartagenero del otro lado del mar

Scene at Marbella[2]

Next to the rocks is God, face up
All in a line the fishermen threw out the long net
And now he lies there with his white eyes looking at the sky
He looks like a lost swimmer
He looks like a big fat fish with a very big tail
But it's only God
swollen with sickly scales
How long has he rolled over the waters?
The curious observe the monstrous fish
Some cut off a piece and take it
                                        home
Others ask themselves if it would be good
to eat food that has been exposed to the elements
                                      for so long

for Juan Marchena, a Cartagenero from the other side of the sea

Destino

Una vez al año, al inicio de las lluvias
la isla es invadida por una ola de cangrejos
que bajan de los montes a aparearse y desovar en el
                                                                                 mar
Se les puede ver enfebrecidos escalando muros
acortando caminos por entre los zaguanes de las casas

Días después los minúsculos recién nacidos abandonan
                                                el agua
e inician un penoso reflujo

Muchos mueren destrozados por los automóviles
o en los malvados juegos de los niños

Pasajes de este misterioso argumento pueden leerse
en los cientos de caparazones dispersos por la isla
O con ciertas variantes que lo magnifican
                                       en algunas páginas de Sófocles

Fate

Once a year, when the rains begin
the island is invaded by a wave of crabs
come down from the woods to mate and lay eggs in the
                                                  sea
You can see them feverishly climbing walls
cutting across roads and entering the hallways of houses

Days later the little ones just born leave
                                    the water
and begin their terrible return

Many are killed by cars
or by children's cruel games

Testament to this mysterious drama can be read
in the hundreds of shells strewn across the island
or in certain variations magnified
                                    in some of Sophocles's pages

Epifanía

Hay algo de monstruosa epifanía en el comprador
                        de oro callejero
su pregón desvalido, su gastado maletín, los empolvados
                                            zapatos
Y luego regatear el precio de una sortija quebrada
a una anciana semioculta detrás de una puerta
Parece un monarca en derrota que vanamente
                        intentara recobrar
restos, fulgores de un dorado imperio

Epiphany

There is something of a monstrous epiphany in the scene of the street peddler
$\qquad\qquad\qquad\qquad\qquad\qquad$ buying gold
his forlorn cry, his worn-out bag, the dust-covered
$\qquad\qquad\qquad\qquad\qquad\qquad\qquad$ shoes
And later to haggle over the price of a broken ringlet
an old woman half-hidden behind a door
He looks like a defeated monarch trying in vain
$\qquad\qquad\qquad\qquad$ to recover
the remains, the glory of a golden empire

De la dificultad para atrapar una mosca

La dificultad para atrapar una mosca
radica en la compleja composición de su ojo

Es el más parecido al ojo de Dios

A través de una red de ocelos diminutos
puede observarte desde todos los ángulos
siempre dispuesta al vuelo

Parece ser que el gran ojo de la mosca
no distingue entre los colores

Probablemente tampoco distinga entre tú
                        que intentas atraparla
y los restos descompuestos en que se posa

On the Difficulty of Catching a Fly

The difficulty of catching a fly
lies in the complicated composition of its eye

It's more like the eye of God

Across a network of little eyes
it can see you from every angle
always ready to flee

It looks like the fly's one big eye
doesn't distinguish between colors

And it probably doesn't distinguish between you
                      who are trying to catch it
and the rest of the garbage it's sitting on

Monólogo de Jonás

Cuando echaron las suertes y los hombres furiosos
                               me arrojaron al mar
creí que era el fin. Pero esto es más que el fin
Si comiera de la carne de este animal durante el resto
                                       de mis días
no alcanzaría la salida. Así es la profundidad
                                 de mi cautiverio

    He transcurrido mucho tiempo sin otro sol
                               que mi propio fuego

A veces me confunde el tumulto de su respiración
la trepidación de sus latidos magnificados por el eco
a través de las muchas cavidades
Como si fuera yo quien respirara
como si mis propios latidos lo inventaran

Acaso sea yo el corazón de la ballena

Jonah's Monologue

When they cast lots and the furious men
                              threw me into the sea
I thought that it was the end. But this is hardly the end
If I were to eat this animal's flesh for the rest
                                    of my days
I would still never get out. Such is the depth
                                of my captivity

      I've spent so much time with no other sun
                                  but my own fire

Sometimes the ferment of his breathing confuses me
the vibration of his heartbeat magnified by its echo
throughout so many cavities
As if I were the one breathing
as if my own heartbeats created him

Perhaps I am the whale's heart

El ángel

Como un trapecista que después
           de un salto mortal
vuelve a buscar la seguridad del trapecio
en el mismo punto del aire donde lo dejara
           y descubre que ese lugar no está allí
que una mano invisible
lo ha empujado hacia otra parte
y en ese sitio hay sólo un hueco, un largo
           tobogán hacia la nada
Sabe que más allá o más acá
o quizás atrás, a sus espaldas, respira
           ese segmento del aire
pero no lo suficientemente cerca de sus pulmones para salvarlo
Sabe que más arriba o más abajo
o quizás delante de sí, ciego a sus ojos
resplandece ese lugar

Entonces cae
comienza a caer
porque comprende que definitivamente es un animal de pelos y pezuñas
y fervorosamente aplaude
a fin de cuentas él es su único y exigente público

The Angel

Like a trapeze artist who after a
               somersault
returns to seek the safety of the trapeze
at the same point in the air where he left it
               and discovers that this spot isn't there
that an invisible hand
has pushed it somewhere else
and in that place there's just a hole, a long
               slide toward nothing
He knows that farther away or closer
or perhaps behind him, at his back, breathes
               that piece of air
but not close enough to his lungs to save him
He knows that above or below
or perhaps in front of him, blind to his eyes
that place shines

Then he falls
begins to fall
because he understands he is definitely an animal of hair and hoofs
and he fervently applauds
after all he is his own unique and discerning audience

Consejo

Elegir con cuidado un punto del aire
Cubrirlo con el cuenco de ambas manos
Arrullarlo
Irlo puliendo en su silencio
Piensa en Dios cuando construyó
su primer caracol o su primer huevo
Acerca el oído para oír como late
Agítalo para ver si responde
Si no puedes con la curiosidad
haz un huequito para mirar adentro
Nada verás. Nada escucharás
Has construido un buen vacío
Ponlo ahora sobre tu corazón y aguarda
confiado el paso de los años

Advice

Carefully choose a point in the air
Cover it with cupped hands
Whisper to it
Polish it in silence
Think about God when he created
his first snail or his first egg
Hold it close to your ear to hear how it sounds
Shake it to see how it responds
If you're overcome with curiosity
make a little hole to look inside
You will see nothing. You will hear nothing
You have made a good hole
Now put it on your heart and wait
confidently throughout the years

Orishas

La muchacha tiene los ojos fijos en un punto
por donde seguramente la música ha abierto
                  un hueco a otra parte
La muchacha agita el muslo derecho y luego desliza
el mismo movimiento al muslo izquierdo
como si hubiera descubierto un modo de trepar
                  por el aire

La muchacha lleva los pies descalzos

Sin duda
el redondo ombligo de la muchacha es ahora
                  el ombligo del mundo

La muchacha baila

Por el hueco abierto por la música
como asomados a una ventana que diera a un patio
                  de vecindad
hermosos guerreros con flautas, antiguas divinidades
                  la contemplan

La muchacha parece reconocerlos

Orishas[3]

The girl has her eyes fixed on a point
through which surely the music has opened
                a hole to another place
The girl shakes her right thigh and then glides
to her left shaking the other
as if she has discovered a way to climb
                through the air

The girl shows her bare feet

Without a doubt
the girl's round navel is now
          the navel of the world

The girl dances

Through the hole opened by the music
like leaning out of a window overlooking the courtyard
beautiful warriors with flutes, ancient divinities
                  gaze at her

The girl seems to recognize them

Sacrificiales

Sacrificials

2007

Lo eterno

Lo eterno está siempre ocurriendo
                        ante tus ojos

Vivo y opaco como una piedra

Y tú debes pulir esa piedra
hasta hacerla un espejo en que poderte mirar
                                  mirándola
Pero entonces el espejo ya será agua y escapará
                                entre tus dedos

Lo eterno está siempre en fuga ante tus ojos

The Eternal

The eternal is always taking place
                               before your eyes

Alive and opaque like a rock

And you should polish that rock
until you make it a mirror so that you can see yourself
                                    looking at it
But then the mirror will already be water and will escape
                                 between your fingers

The eternal is always disappearing before your eyes

El carroñero

El carroñero hace bien su tarea:
mondar el hueso, purificarlo de la pútrida
                              excrecencia
En algún lugar de la vida, algo
hace exactamente lo contrario: cubre el hueso
empuja la oscura floración de la carne
A su extraño modo
el carroñero también trabaja en la resurrección
                          de los muertos

The Scavenger

The scavenger does his work well:
to peel the bone, to purify it of the putrid
                              excrescence
Somewhere else, something else
does exactly the opposite: it covers the bone
provokes the dark flowering of the flesh
In an odd way
the scavenger also works to resurrect
                              the dead

Sicología de la madreperla

En algún oscuro momento a la madreperla
le es dado saber
que el mal que la aqueja no es un intruso
                             sino su raíz
Por tanto no puede expulsarlo
Entonces
amorosa, duramente
decide arrullarlo en su nácar
Después lo abisma en su seno
Después lo convierte en su segunda raíz
Después lo olvida
Después
le cuesta trabajo reconocerlo en el poema
que aparece publicado en alguna revista

Psychology of the Mother-of-Pearl

At an unknown moment the mother-of-pearl
comes to realize
the evil that afflicts her isn't an intruder
                         but her root
So she can't expel it
Then
lovingly, harshly
she decides to cradle it in her nacre[1]
Afterward she buries it in her bosom
Afterward she transforms it into her second root
Afterward she forgets it
Afterward
she has trouble recognizing it in a poem
published in some magazine

Para un manual del inquisidor

No mirarás la mirada de la bruja
prescribe el *Malleus Maleficarum*

Podrás paladear la sal de su carne mientras le aplicas el torno
Podrás disfrutar la flor áspera de su grito
Podrás olfatear su miedo mientras descoyuntas sus miembros

Pero *no mirarás su mirada*

Pues allí habita su más poderoso hechizo
Si lo hicieras estarías en sus manos, en sus ojos
Serías víctima entonces, de la temible compasión

    Y habrás perdido todo tu esfuerzo para salvar su alma

For the Inquisitor's Manual

You will not return the witch's gaze
prescribes the *Malleus Maleficarum*[2]

You will be able to savor the salt of her flesh while you apply the drill
You will be able to relish the jagged edges of her screams
You will be able to catch a whiff of her fear while you break her limbs

But *you will not look her in the eye*

Because therein lies her most powerful spell
If you were to look you would be in her hands, in her eyes
You would then be a victim of terrifying compassion

    And all the work to save her soul will have been in vain

Mantarraya

Por algún divertido arreglo
los dos muchachos han dividido en dos la mantarraya
como si fuera una hoja de papel
y ahora cada uno lleva su parte colgando de la mano

Ya nada queda de la gracia que el animal
                                    exhibe en los acuarios
Ondeando, sumergiéndose, elevándose en el agua
todo su cuerpo como dos extrañas alas

Mientras la ofrecen a lo largo de la playa los dos muchachos
aseguran que con ella se prepara un excelente
                                    y vigorizante cocido

Las dos partes siguen vivas

A veces una de ellas levemente se estremece y aletea
                                    como si una parte reclamara la otra

O como si conservara alguna oscura memoria de su vuelo

Manta Ray

Because of some mischievous plot
the two guys have cut the manta ray in two
as if it were a sheet of paper
and now each one carries away his part in his hand

Nothing remains of the grace that the animal
                                          exhibits in aquariums
Rippling, submerging, floating in the water
its entire body like two strange wings

Meanwhile the two guys try to sell it on the beach
They claim that you can use it to make a delicious
                                          and arousing stew

The two parts are still alive

Sometimes one of them slightly shudders and flutters
                          as if one part is looking for the other

Or as if it harbors some faint memory of its flight

Poema con pez y garcetas

Las garcetas blancas rizan con sus patas la superficie del lago
Lo hacen a intervalos rítmicos mientras planean a baja altura
Al fondo, bordeados de mangles, polvorientos baldíos
Cuesta pensar que no se trata de algo más que un juego
                                          o una danza
En realidad, con esas periódicas caricias al agua, las garcetas
                                        buscan atraer a los peces
que literalmente
vienen a morir a sus pies, bajo sus eficaces picos

(bajo el agua el goloso pez solo ha visto otro pez
más pequeño que espejea y salta brevemente sobre el agua)

No hay gratuidad en ese bello gesto como quisieras, alma mía

Ni tan solo belleza alguna en ese bello gesto
Solo tú y el iluso pez que se confunden

El resto es literatura—te dices conclusiva

Hay, sin embargo, un extraño fulgor en la muerte
una misteriosa belleza en un pez que viene a morir
en medio de las aguas insomnes de un poema—añades finalmente
Y el poema y el pez te lo agradecen

Poem with Fish and Egrets

The white egrets ripple the lake's surface with their feet
at rhythmic intervals while gliding low
At the far end, bordered by mangroves, dusty wastelands
It's hard to think of it as something more than a game
                               or a dance
In reality, with the periodic caressing of the water, the egrets
                               try to attract the fish
that literally
come to die at their feet, in their lethal beaks

(below the water the greedy fish have only seen other smaller fish
that shimmer and briefly leap out of the water)

There is no caprice in that graceful gesture as you would like, my soul

Nor even beauty in that graceful gesture
Only you and the naïve fish got confused

The rest is literature—you tell yourself conclusively

There is, nevertheless, a strange glow in death
a mysterious beauty in a fish that comes to die
in the middle of the sleepless waters of a poem—you add finally
And the poem and the fish appreciate you

Cotidiana

La hermana pasa lentamente la escoba sobre el pequeño tumulto
de las hormigas
y no cesa de asombrarse de lo rápidas que acudieron
al saltamontes inesperadamente caído del techo
—Parece que supieran—dice
Cuánta minúscula y moviente voracidad sobre el cuerpo muerto
Cuánto vértigo de pinzas trincando, desgarrando, cargando
victoriosamente el animalejo

—Algo las llama—insiste sabiamente la hermana

Yo nada digo
Yo aparto los pies y dejo barrer
mientras miro la desorientación de las hormigas
que ahora no parecen saber tanto

Everyday

The sister slowly passes the broom over the little frenzy
of ants
and never ceases to be amazed at how fast they found
the grasshopper that fell unexpectedly from the roof
—It looks as though they knew—she says
So small and so voracious moving over the dead body
So many whirling claws picking, ripping, victoriously carrying away
that critter

—Something calls them—the sister wisely insists

I don't say anything
I move my feet and let her sweep
while I look at the ants' confusion
now they don't look like they know so much

Dactiloscopia

Justo cuando mueves el hilo con el dedo
aparece la araña con todas sus patas, su abdomen, sus pelos
y sus ojos casi ciegos

Examina atentamente tu dedo
los meandros sin centro aparente de tu huella
la uña curvada y agresiva, la pequeña mugre que en ella
                                            se acumula
Los pellejos que se han endurecido a ambos lados y parecen
pequeños cuernos, es lo que más familiar le resulta
Pero no acierta a intuir el resto misterioso en que te extiendes
con todas tus patas, tu abdomen, tus pelos y tus ojos casi ciegos

Le resultas una presa extraña

Demasiado evidente para ignorarla
demasiado hipotética para comerla

Decide que tú debes ser Dios o algo parecido
y se agazapa de nuevo a esperar un bicho menos complicado
más limpio y digerible

Dactyloscopy[3]

Just when you move the thread with your finger
a spider appears with all its legs, its abdomen, its hair
and nearly blind eyes

It carefully examines your finger
The apparent centerless meanders of your fingerprint
the curved and aggressive fingernail, the little dirt
                                            that accumulates
The skin that has hardened on both sides and looks like
little horns, that's what it's most familiar with
but it can't guess the mysterious remnant in which you expand
With your feet, your abdomen, your hair and your nearly blind eyes

You're strange prey

Too evident to ignore
too hypothetical to eat

It decides that you should be God or something similar
and it crouches again to wait for a creature less complicated
cleaner and digestible

De la levedad

Érase un alma tan leve que cuando murió su cuerpo
era tal su levedad que pasó sin detenerse ante la Puerta del cielo

Al menos eso fue lo que creyó el Guardián de la Puerta

Y el Guardián de la Puerta alarmado
temiendo que fuera a dar al Abismo o Vórtice de la nada
le sugirió que, a modo de plomadas, dejara caer palabras pesadas
Y el alma leve dijo: ceiba, argamasa, potala, escaparate

Pero siguió levitando

Y el Guardián de la Puerta le sugirió que probara con malas palabras
Y el alma leve dijo palabras crapulosas
que la censura celeste me impide repetir

Pero siguió levitando

Y el Guardián de la Puerta le sugirió que probara con palabras inmundas
Y el alma leve dijo palabras inmundas
que el asco me hace imposible repetir

Y finalmente el alma leve se perdió de vista
ante la mirada desolada del Guardián de la Puerta

El Guardián de la Puerta
que era en realidad Sir Isaac Newton en apariencia de Guardián de la Puerta
no lograría comprender que *per saecula saeculorum* nada sabría
sobre el libre vuelo o caída de las almas en el espacio angélico
ni mucho menos entender
que en eso consistía su propio y exclusivo círculo del infierno

Of Levity

There once was a soul so faint that when the body died
she was light enough to pass through the gates of heaven without stopping

At least that was what the Gatekeeper thought

And the Gatekeeper was scared
Fearing that he was to be thrown into the abyss or vortex of nothingness
He suggested that, like plumb lines, the soul should drop heavy words
And the faint soul said: oak tree, cement, anchor, armoire

But she continued to rise

And the Gatekeeper suggested to her to try profanity
And the faint soul said curse words
that the celestial censor stops me from repeating

But she continued to rise

And the Gatekeeper suggested to her that she try filthy words
And the faint soul said filthy words
that were so foul that I can't repeat them

And finally the faint soul was gone from sight
lost to the Gatekeeper's desolate gaze

The Gatekeeper
who was really Sir Isaac Newton disguised as the Gatekeeper
wouldn't ever understand *per saecula saeculorum*[4] nothing is known
about free flight or fallen souls in the angelic space
much less did he understand
that there he would find his own circle of hell

Cinegética

No hay gacelas por estas tierras
Pero existe el saíno
La carne del saíno—dicen
sabe tan bien como la de la gacela
Es verdad que no tiene prestigio literario
pero ambas hacen igual a la garra del tigre

De todos modos sangrará el poema

No hay que olvidar, en todo caso, que después de Borges
el tigre tiene tanto prestigio literario como la gacela

Ignoro si aún existen tigres en estas tierras
En todo caso habrá cazador

Gacela, tigre y saíno hacen igual a la garra del cazador

De todos modos sangrará el poema

El saíno carece del oro de los tigres y de la gracia de la gacela

La muerte asimismo carece de ambas cosas
Y tiene menos prestigio literario que el poema
Pero es real

Tiene las siete vidas del gato, más la del saíno, la gacela, el tigre
                                       el cazador y el poeta

Todo eso para poder habitar en la sangrante irrealidad del poema

Cynegetics[5]

There are no gazelles here
But the peccary[6] does live here
The meat of the peccary—they say
is as good as that of the gazelle
It's true that it doesn't have literary prestige
but it's all the same in the tiger's claws

Anyway the poem will bleed

There is no forgetting, in any case, that after Borges[7]
the tiger has so much more literary prestige like the gazelle

I ignore the possibility that tigers may still live here
In any case there will be a hunter

Gazelle, tiger, and peccary are all the same in the claws of the hunter

Anyway the poem will bleed

The peccary lacks the tiger's gold and the gazelle's grace

Death also lacks both things
And it has less literary prestige than the poem
But it's real

It has the cat's seven lives, plus that of the peccary, the gazelle, the tiger
                                the hunter and the poet

All this to be able to inhabit the bloody illusion of the poem

De los sólidos platónicos

> Todo lo sólido se desvanece en el aire
> —*Marx-shall Berman*

Un amigo me obsequió
los sólidos platónicos hechos en frágil cartulina

Me los dejó en una pequeña caja sobre el escritorio de mi oficina
acompañado de una nota:
esta cajita contiene el alfabeto del mundo
con ellos están construidos la piedra, la geometría inversa
del cangrejo, los movimientos de un atleta
        y hasta los sueños

Por algún rato observo los objetos cuidadosamente

La esfera, en verdad, es francamente luminosa
El icosaedro, con sus veinte rostros, tiene algo de araña, de flor
                monstruosa
Y qué decir de la enigmática elementalidad de la pirámide

En fin
a falta de un manual de instrucciones decidí colocarlos en un frutero

A los pocos días desaparecieron y fueron a dar a la basura
pues, la señora que me hace los oficios consideró que las nuevas frutas
definitivamente estaban en el lugar equivocado

To be or not to be, como decía Platón, equivoqué pensativo

Entonces decido ponerle ese epígrafe al poema

Of the Platonic Solids[8]

> All that is solid melts into air.
> —*Marx-shall Berman*[9]

A friend gave me
the platonic solids made of fragile cardboard

He left them for me in a little box on the desk in my office
along with a note:
this little box contains the alphabet of the world
with them are created the rock, the inverse geometry
of the crab, the movements of an athlete
                and even dreams

For some time, I observe the objects carefully

The sphere, in truth, is really bright
The icosahedron,[10] with its twenty faces has something of the spider, of a
                                          monstrous flower
And what about the enigmatic simplicity of the pyramid

Anyway
without an instruction manual I decided to put them in a fruit bowl

A few days later they disappeared and were put in the trash
because the lady who cleans my house thought the new fruit
definitely was in the wrong place

To be or not to be, as Plato says, I thought incorrectly

So I decide to put this epigraph in the poem

Contra Parménides o la mariapalito

La inmovilidad de la mariapalito podría haber dado
a ciertos filósofos
razonamientos más convincentes que el de la flecha
o aquel otro más divulgado de Aquiles y la tortuga

Ella no lo sabe
Si lo supiera luciría más filosófica de lo que parece

Todo llama a su transformación, nada quiere permanecer fijado a su ser
el poema pide ser prosa
la piedra pide ser agua,
el horizonte pide ser línea vertical

Pero la inmóvil mariapalito solo quiere ser mariapalito

Muy flaquísima Señora del límite, del umbral
no sabe que, en realidad, ella es el más fino argumento
contra el estatismo que su apariencia pregona
que, sin que lo haya pedido, siendo un insecto de cuatro patas
algo dentro de ella, algo remoto, la mueve a ser palito

Por eso se llama así

Pero eso tampoco parece saberlo la mariapalito

Against Parmenides or the Little Stick Bug

The stillness of the stick bug could have given
certain philosophers
more convincing reasoning than that of the arrow
or that more famous of Achilles and the tortoise[11]

She doesn't know it
If she knew, she would look more philosophical than she does

Everything calls for transformation, nothing wants to remain fixed to its own being
the poem asks to be prose
the rock asks to be water
the horizon asks to be a vertical line

But the unmoving stick bug only wants to be a stick bug

Our very thin Lady of limits, of the threshold
she doesn't know that, in reality, she is the most refined argument
against the stillness her appearance announces
that which she didn't ask for, being an insect with four legs
something inside of her, something remote, moves her to be a stick

That's why she has that name

But the stick bug doesn't seem to know

El arcángel

A los escasos visitantes de mi estudio ha extrañado con frecuencia, el lugar vacío o informe a los pies del Arcángel, donde debiera figurar el demonio. Es una imagen de bulto realizada por algún anónimo tallista y adquirida por azar en algún almacén de objetos religiosos.

Yo les comento que, en contraste con la prodigiosa representación del ángel, el artífice había sido poco generoso con el Tentador y, por solo gozarme en la contemplación de lo bello, le pedí al vendedor que lo excluyera del conjunto como condición para comprarlo.

Tantos años en su compañía. Ciertamente, se han ido opacando sus vivos colores de legionario; no obstante conserva su esplendor.

Los visitantes, casi siempre, han acabado haciendo alguna graciosa ocurrencia sobre mi esteticismo. Alguno llegó a sugerir la idea de que yo, más bien, había pretendido llevar simbólicamente a sus últimas consecuencias la labor de exterminio encomendada al Celeste.

Mi amigo Alfonso Múnera no ha desestimado esta hipótesis. Pero opina que en ese acto de mutilación, más allá de cualquier manía estetizante, habría operado la paradójica poética de la inocencia del maestro Rojas Herazo cuya obra sabe que admiro.

Sin duda es poco caritativa la imagen del caído condenado a contemplar por la eternidad la espada fulgurante del vencedor.

Pero el asunto posee repercusiones no sospechadas según me revelara recientemente el Arcángel en ocasión que ahora ilumina en mi memoria.

Dulce e irónico me interrogó aquella tarde sosteniendo en las manos las *Elegías del Duino*. Las había estado hojeando como al descuido mientras yo dibujaba.

—¿Sabes qué condición ontológica es más terrible que la de un ángel?
—No se me ocurre, respondí intrigado
—Un ángel al que han separado de su demonio
—¿Ignorabas que eran las atroces alas del mal lo que sostenía mi purísimo vuelo?

Yo lo observo desde el radiante corredor de las campanas amarillas, lentamente apenumbrándose en el silencio de su abierto secreto. Me apena su orfandad.

Cada día se debilitan más sus primitivos colores. Cada vez se hace más visible su opacamiento. Los visitantes ya comienzan a advertirlo. Un día cualquiera se desvanecerá. Un día cualquiera entraré al estudio y solo encontraré sobre el muro los desvaídos trazos de una mancha de luz.

Nada de esto último he comentado a los visitantes. Aprovecho este espacio en *Sacrificiales* para contarlo.

a Edda Armas, mensajera

The Archangel

The few visitors to my studio have often missed it, the empty space or the shape at the Archangel's feet, where the figure of the devil should have been. It's a massive image made by some anonymous sculptor and acquired by chance in some store for religious objects.

I tell them that, in contrast to the wondrous representation of the angel, the craftsman hadn't been so generous with the Tempter and, only to amuse myself in the contemplation of the beautiful thing, I asked the seller to exclude it from the set as a condition of purchase.

So many years in its company. Certainly its vibrant colors have darkened; nevertheless it has kept its splendor.

Visitors have almost always ended up mocking me about myaesthetics. Some even suggested that I had intended to bring symbolically to its conclusion the work entrusted to this heavenly being.

My friend Alfonso Múnera has not ruled out this hypothesis. But he thinks that this act of mutilation, apart from whatever aesthetic obsession, could have been a part of the paradoxical poetics of the innocent by master Rojas Herazo[12] whose work he knows I admire.

Without a doubt, it's uncharitable, the image of the fallen condemned to contemplate for eternity the victor's brilliant sword.

But the matter poses unanticipated repercussions according to what the archangel revealed recently to me on an occasion that now stands out in my memory.

Sweet and ironic he questioned me that afternoon holding in his hands the *Elegies of Duino*.[13] He had been leafing through it while I was drawing.

—Do you know what ontological condition is worse than that of an angel?
—It didn't occur to me, I responded puzzled
—An angel who has been separated from his demon
—Didn't you know that it was evil's awful wings that sustained my pure flight?

I watch him from the radiant hall of yellow bells, lingering in the silence of his open secret. I'm sorry that he's an orphan.

Every day his original colors become weaker. Every day his fading becomes more obvious. The visitors have already begun to warn me. Any day now he will disappear. Any day now I will enter the studio and only see on the wall the washed-out stroke of a sunbeam.

I haven't said any of this last part to the visitors. I use this space in *Sacrificials*.

> *for Edda Armas, messenger*

Mirando una estampa de Santa Lucía en un texto hagiográfico

Los ojos, siguiendo la tradicional iconografía
reposan sobre un plato, como dos peces muertos
Ojos grandes y soñadores
Me digo imaginando las cuencas vacías

Tan grandes que por ellos debió caber el mundo, toda la carne
                                                  y sus demonios

me sopla al oído mi fiel demonio de cabecera
Yo lo espanto y él se va con el rabo entre las piernas
al fondo de la habitación que compartimos

Patrona de las modistillas y de los sastres, reza al pie de la estampa

Y acaso de los voyeristas, comenta mi demonio de cabecera
Y arrecia el ataque
acudiendo a una cita apócrifa de san Isidoro
y añadiendo no sé qué gracias y desgracias de cierto
ojo divulgadas por Quevedo
Y para que no quede dudas acerca de qué está hablando
rubrica todo esto con una sonora ventosidad

Los dos peces muertos no se dan por aludidos

Yo finjo ignorarlo y paso juiciosamente a otra página del libro
Pero él sabe que ha hecho bien su trabajo, y sonríe
                              mientras lame su pelaje

Looking at a Portrait of Saint Lucia[14] in a Hagiographic Text

The eyes, following the iconographic tradition
rest on the plate, like two dead fish
Big dreamy eyes
I say to myself imagining the empty eye sockets

So big that the entire world could fit in them, all the flesh
and its demons

my faithful demon blows in my ear
I frighten him and he runs away with his tail between his legs
to the far side of the room that we share

Patron saint of seamstresses and tailors, written at the feet of the portrait

And maybe of the voyeurs, comments my faithful demon
And the attack gets worse
going to an apocryphal quote of Saint Isidore[15]
and adding I don't know about the grace or disgrace of a certain
eye revealed by Quevedo[16]
And so that there's no doubt about what he is saying
he punctuates it with a loud fart

The two dead fish don't get the joke

And I pretend to ignore him and slowly turn the page
But he knows that he has done his job, and he smiles
               as he licks his fur

En el zoológico

Lo siniestro (*Unheimlich*) es todo lo que debiendo permanecer secreto, oculto, no obstante se ha manifestado
—*Schelling*

Quizás no haya más viva y precisa expresión
de lo siniestro que el trasero del mandril

Por definición
una vez que lo siniestro se ha manifestado no podemos evitar pertenecerle
                                        entrar en su tortuoso juego
    De allí ese comportamiento ambiguo y hasta divertido de los visitantes del
                                                                                     zoo
cuando llegan a la zona de los mandriles
Una vez que el ojo ha hallado
las conocidas y chocantes callosidades posteriores de estos simios
—y es como si secretamente hubiera estado buscando—
en movimiento de péndulo
o en vértigo de lo simultáneo
los apropia y expulsa como su objeto. De allí en adelante
los visitantes mirarán de reojo
como si estando no estuvieran
o como si quisieran que cuando voltearan a verlos hubieran desaparecido
pero solo acaso, extrañamente, para poder seguir observándolos a su gusto
                                                   en la imaginación

    Esto sucede sobre todo con las muchachas. Sobre todo con las muchachas
                                      de bellos y lustrosos traseros
    Sobre todo si van en grupo las muchachas
cuchicheando entre sí y luego apartándose y retornando
siempre ruborosas retornando las muchachas

    Y allí estarán esperando en ofensivo contrapunto los mandriles
    La escandalosa floración visceral desbordando sus límites
ofreciéndose obscena a los ojos del visitante

Los mandriles
por supuesto, no han leído a Schelling ni a Freud ni mucho menos a Bataille
como tú, mi ilustrado lector
Pero algo deben intuir
de su papel en la complicada economía espiritual del visitante
No en balde son ramas de un mismo árbol
Por eso se pavonean exhibiendo sus repulsivas corolas-culos

Algo deben sospechar del asunto
cuando irritantes dan la espalda y comienzan
                                       a observarlo con su gran ojo
                                   inescrutable, único
Acaso en ese momento el visitante alcanzará a comprender
que no es ese ojo paródico del mandril, ni el mandril mismo, sino algo distinto
lo Absolutamente Otro
es decir, lo íntimamente tú afuera respirando, desbordado de ti
lo que lo mira

Lo siniestro
ciertamente nos constituye y nos habita

Pero sobre eso ya se han ocupado suficientemente los teóricos
Yo solo quería hablar de los visitantes del zoológico, sobre todo de las
                                                      muchachas
de los bellos y lustrosos traseros de las muchachas

In the Zoo

> The uncanny (*Unheimlich*) is all that should remain secret, hidden, but
> nevertheless it has become manifest
> —*Schelling*[17]

Maybe there's no more vibrant and accurate expression
of the uncanny than the backside of the mandrill[18]

By definition
once the uncanny is manifested we cannot avoid being possessed by it
                to enter its tortuous game
Hence the ambiguous and even amusing behavior of the zoo's visitors
when they get to the mandrills' area
Once the eye has found
the familiar and shocking callused posterior of those apes
—and it's as if the eye had been furtively looking for it—
moving like a pendulum
or simultaneously up and down
the eye takes in and expels them. From then on
the visitors look out of the corner of their eyes
as if they were and were not there
or as if they wished that when they turned to look at them they would have
                                                              disappeared
but strangely, so that the visitors could continue to see them in their
                                                              imagination
                                          for their amusement

    This happens mostly with the girls. Especially with the girls
                                with beautiful and shiny butts
    Especially if the girls are in a group
    whispering to each other and going back and forth
    always blushing upon their return

    And there the mandrills will be waiting in their offensive pose
    The scandalous visceral bloom bursting its limits
    offering itself obscenely to the visitors' eye

The mandrills
of course, have not read Schelling nor Freud[19] and least of all Bataille[20]
like you, my illustrious reader
But they should intuit something
of their role in the visitors' complicated spiritual economy
It's not in vain that they are branches of the same tree
And so they display their repulsive corolla-asses

They should be suspicious of something in this scenario
when irritated they turn their backs and begin to watch with the great eye
                                            inscrutable, unique

Perhaps at this moment the visitor begins to understand
that it's not the mandrill's parodic eye, nor the mandrill himself, but something different
the Absolute Other
that's to say, the most intimate you outside of yourself, breathing, overflowing, watching

The uncanny
certainly makes us and lives within us
but the theorists have already exhausted that subject

I only wanted to talk about the zoo's visitors, about all of the girls
about their beautiful and shiny butts

Sacrificial

El carnicero se va en lenguas
hablando de las bondades de cada una de las carnes del animal. Casi saborea las palabras
El cliente señala difuso un punto en el dibujo que se exhibe en la pared
donde sabiamente aparece seccionada la res en sus diferentes partes
para golosa guía del comiente
Sin duda el comido no ha sido consultado sobre la publicidad
$$\text{de sus vísceras}$$

Ah, el comiente
Con sus pulcros caninos, sus radiantes incisivos y sus 356 molares

Pero hay algo de torva beatitud en la demora con que, a veces, el carnicero
rasga una entretela, contempla al trasluz y retira delicadamente
$$\text{un trozo de pellejo}$$

Quizás, en esos instantes, alguien dentro de él ensueña:
un día cualquiera
un distraído arcángel, confundido en el tiempo, vendrá y me relevará
de este sucio mandil, detendrá mi mano en el aire de la mañana y dirá
fulgurante:
basta, ya tu fe ha sido probada

El cliente, recostado en el mostrador, lo mira con expectante fulgor
Y el ensoñador quisiera indagar: ¿acaso eres tú mi liberador?
pero dice oferente: ¿palomilla o punta de nalga?
Ahora, el carnicero tararea indolente mientras pule sus enormes cuchillos

a Juan Calzadilla

Sacrificial

The butcher trades in tongues
every day talking about the benefits of each animal's flesh. He can almost taste the words
The customer points vaguely to a point on the drawing that hangs on the wall
where the beef is cut up smartly into different parts
a drawing guide for the eater
Undoubtedly the eaten has not been consulted about advertising
                                      its viscera

Ah, the eater
With his immaculate canines, his radiant incisors and his 356 molars

But there is something of a grim blessing in the care with which, at times, the butcher
tears the entrails, contemplates the light and delicately removes
                                      pieces of hide

Maybe, in these moments, someone inside of him dreams:
any day
a confused archangel, lost in time, will come and relieve me
from this dirty apron, raise my hand in the morning air and say to me
fulgently:
enough, your faith has been proved

The customer, leaning on the counter, looks at him with an expectant gaze
And the dreamer would like to ask: Are you my liberator?
but he offers: steak or a piece of the rump?
Now, the butcher hums lazily while he sharpens his enormous knives

   for Juan Calzadilla

Un paco-paco

El paco-paco canta con las patas traseras
Recuerdo un paco-paco que alegró la noche a todos
los niños de la cuadra porque confundimos su canto con los crótalos
                                       de una cascabel
Con palos y mochas la buscamos entre los matojos
hasta que descubrimos el engaño

En realidad
Él ya nos había descubierto antes con sus grandes ojos
                                       de mirar el mundo
sin entender nuestra alharaca, y entonando el más perfecto
                                       de los silencios
que alguna vez hubiéramos escuchado

Pero este paco-paco que ahora miro sobre la ramita
                                       del matarratón
ha perdido una pata. Su ambigua pata para el salto
                                       para el canto

Es curioso que la voz de un animal esté en sus patas

Miro al animalito tratar en vano de frotar la una
                                       con la no-otra pata
y me es inevitable evocar el conocido epigrama zen
que enigmáticamente se pregunta: ¿Cómo es el sonido de una sola mano
                                       que aplaude?
¿Existe, acaso, ese sonido?
Y tú, Bustos, tratas también de frotar, de desplegar tus dos patas
                                       traseras, tu ala única

y entonces escuchas (o imaginas o crees o quieres escuchar)
ese otro insondable sonido que te responde

desde qué matojo

desde qué inescrutable esquina del paisaje, desde qué
silencio

A Cricket

The cricket sings with his hind legs
I remember a cricket that cheered up the night for us all
the children on our block because we confused his song with the rattle of the
                                                    rattlesnakes
We looked for it with sticks and machetes in the thicket
until we discovered his trick

Actually
He had already found us with his big eyes
                                  to look at the world
without understanding our fuss, and singing the most perfect
                                      of the silences
that we would have ever heard

But this cricket that I see now on the little branch
                                of the matarratón tree
has lost a leg. His other leg for jumping
                        for the song

It's curious that an animal's voice is in its legs
I look at the little animal trying in vain to rub the one
                                against the missing leg
and I naturally recall the well-known Zen epigram
that enigmatically asks: What is the sound of one hand
                              clapping?
Does that sound even exist?
And you, Bustos, you also try to rub, to show your
                              hind legs, your only wing

and then you hear (or you imagine or think or want to hear)
this other mysterious sound that responds to you

from what thicket

from what obscure corner of the woods from what
silence

Poema probable

El asunto podría ocurrir así:
El ser se retrae
Todo le es trance, desconocimiento
           extática vigilia
El oculto don de las alas que ha estado escrito en algún lugar
de su crujiente biología, se despliega

Grieta, latencia, derrumbe

Al ser todo esto le es extraño
como si en su interior alguien lo estuviera soñando

Al final
la libélula que ya no se reconoce en la vieja escoria de su cuerpo
                                   se eleva
y la minuciosa caparazón, abandonada
como se abandonan los andamios y aparejos usados en una construcción
colgará en algún ramaje del jardín

Probablemente cuelgue muy frágil y el viento acabe arrastrándola
Probablemente se deshaga en las manos curiosas de un niño
Probablemente tú, podando los ramajes, la encuentres
Probablemente este hallazgo te plantee un imperioso enigma:
¿Qué misteriosa vocación de altura lleva a la larva de la libélula a dejar de ser
una criatura de agua para convertirse en una criatura de aire?
Probablemente se te ocurra que este mínimo esqueleto es una especie de fósil
que, de algún modo, bien pudiera ofrecerte algún indicio
acerca de la arqueología del alma o la sigilosa alquimia de tus alas

Y aquí, probablemente, se detiene el poema
Y prosigue su vuelo el deseo, el más puro esplendor de la fábula

Probable Poem

It could happen like this:
The being withdraws
Everything for him is trance, ignorance
                ecstatic wakefulness
The hidden gift of wings written somewhere
in his rigid biology, unfolds

Crack, latency, collapse

To the being all of that is strange
as if in his interior someone were dreaming him

Finally
the dragonfly no longer recognizable in the old waste of his body
                                                          rises
and the meticulous carapace, abandoned
as the scaffolding and rigging used in construction are abandoned
it will hang in some branch in the garden

Probably it hangs so fragile and the wind finally drags it away
Probably crushed in a child's curious hands
Probably while pruning the branches, you find it
Probably finding it poses for you a real problem:
What mysterious higher power takes the larva of the dragonfly and transforms it from a creature of water into a creature of air?
Probably it occurs to you that this tiny skeleton is some kind of fossil
that, somehow, it might offer you some sign
something like the archaeology of the soul or the sly alchemy of your wings

And here, probably, the poem stops
And desire continues its flight, the fable's purest expression

La capa de juegos

No todos han tenido una capa de juegos
Yo tuve una. La heredé de mi hermana Deyanira

Era una tela bermeja que una vez mi hermana lució en una procesión
en que iba vestida de Santa Catalina por ser la muchacha más graciosa del
                                                                                                        pueblo

Yo me metía debajo de la capa y la desvaída y calurosa realidad que me
                                                                                                         rodeaba
se convertía en tienda sioux, follaje gigante de árboles, alcázar
o—preferiblemente—cálido iglú del cual salía a cazar focas en medio de un
intenso
paraje de intrigante blancura

La hermosa tela finalmente acabó colgando de algún clavo en algún
lugar de la casa y luego se hizo jirones

A veces pienso
que la poesía es esa capa de juegos a la que siempre vuelvo o de la que acaso
nunca he salido
Otras
que la poesía es, más bien, esa pesada foca muerta que no alcanzó
a llegar al mar

Mi hermana—siempre compasiva, siempre benévola—cree
que la poesía está más cerca de esa extraña pelota de colores
que todas las focas del mundo llevan sobre el hocico
y que todos los niños caza-focas desean poseer bajo sus capas de juego

Bien!, exclama el pequeño caza-focas: ahora tengo claro parte del enigma
pero, aún no acabo de entender por qué debo matar a la foca

Mi hermana Deyanira—siempre compasiva, siempre benévola—sonríe
desde algún lugar del misterio

    a Laura-Palmera

The Magic Cape

Not everyone has had a magic cape
I had one. I inherited it from my sister Deyanira

It was a red cloth she wore once in a procession
for being the prettiest girl in town; she went dressed as Santa Catalina[21]

I put on the cape and the faded and bland reality that engulfed me
became a Sioux tent, giant foliage of trees, a fortress
or—preferably—a warm igloo from which I left to hunt seals in the middle of a
landscape of intense and ineffable whiteness

The beautiful cloth finally was hung on a nail in some
corner of the house and later just fell apart

Sometimes I think
poetry is a magic cape to which I return or from which
I have never left
Other times
poetry is, rather, a heavy dead seal that couldn't get back to
the sea

My sister—always compassionate, always kind—believes
poetry is closer to that strange ball of colors
all the seals of the world carry on their snouts
and all the child seal-hunters want to have under their magic capes

Great! exclaims the little seal-hunter: now I understand one part of the puzzle
but I still don't understand why I should kill the seal

My sister Deyanira—always compassionate, always kind—smiles
from some mysterious place

   for Laura-Palmera

Muerte y levitación de la ballena

Death and Levitation of the Whale

2010

Cuento

Me pregunto: ¿Por qué escribo poesía?
Y desde algún lugar del misterioso bosque
(de ese otro cuento que en vano estoy tratando
                de escribir en este poema)
responde el lobo
moviendo socrático la peluda cola:
—Para conocerte mejor

Story

I ask myself: Why do I write poetry?
And from some place in the mysterious forest
(from the other story I'm trying
               to write in vain in this poem)
the wolf answers
moving his furry tail in a Socratic manner:
—All the better to know you

Observación hecha desde el hemisferio izquierdo del cerebro

Es probable que Dios no exista
Esto en realidad carece de importancia

Más interesante es saber
que existe el hemisferio derecho del cerebro
cuya función es soñarlo

Observation Made from the Left Hemisphere of the Brain

It's likely God doesn't exist
That's actually unimportant

More interesting is knowing
That there's the right hemisphere of the brain
whose function is to dream Him

Del cangrejo ermitaño

Rara costumbre la del cangrejo ermitaño

Se le va la vida buscando caparazones de otros
moluscos, latas, recipientes vacíos
toda suerte de objetos cóncavos abandonadas por sus
antiguos huéspedes para instalarse en ellos

Es posible que todo se deba
a una compulsión turística por la novedad

O a un síndrome de inestabilidad casi metafísica

O a simple ejercicio peripatético de quien tiene
        demasiadas patas que ejercitar

¿O habrá algo más de fondo en todo esto?

Quizás convenga preguntar
al secreto cangrejo ermitaño que habita
            en cada uno de nosotros

Ese que, sin duda, acaba de escribir este poema

Of the Hermit Crab

The hermit crab has a strange habit.

He spends his life looking for the shells of other
mollusks, cans, empty containers
all kinds of concave objects abandoned by their old
guests so that he can move in

It's possible that all of this is due to
a touristic impulse for novelty

Or a syndrome of a near metaphysical instability

Or a simple peripatetic experiment for someone who has
                        too many legs to exercise

Or is there more to it than that?

Perhaps it's best to ask
the secret hermit crab that lives
                in each one of us

It's he, no doubt, who just wrote this poem

Euclidiano

El ángulo de visión del ser humano se ubica en el rango
de los 180°
Los otros 180° corresponden al dominio de su sombra

Caso cerrado. Círculo concluso

En realidad, no es tan simple la cosa. Veamos:

Está la sombra visible
Mas, ¿y el dominio de la sombra invisible?
Porque toda sombra tiene su propia sombra
                 bien advierten Juarroz y Luis Vidales

¿Y el dominio fronterizo del espejo
que se divierte duplicando los espacios e invirtiendo a su modelo?

Por otra parte, visto desde la óptica de la sombra visible
tú eres la verdadera sombra visible

Además, correspondientes a los distintos ángulos de visión
de tus numerosos yoes, fragmentos de yoes y otros fantasmas
                        que te habitan
habrá infinitas circunferencias—mundos
con sus respectivos 180° al sol
                180° a la sombra
y sus consecuentes subdominios de sombras invisibles
                      y sombras-espejos

Todo esto, sin duda, parece un mal sueño de Euclides

En todo caso cuando Euclides despierte
el monstruo seguirá allí

    a Lázaro, a Esteban
    mirando un filme de Kim Ki Duk

Euclidian[1]

The angle of vision for a human being is located at the level
of 180°
The other 180° correspond to the domain of the shadow

Case closed. End of discussion

Actually, it's not that simple. Let's see:

The shadow is visible
But what about the domain of the invisible shadow?
Because the entire shadow has its own shadow
      warn Juarroz[2] and Luis Vidales[3]

And what about the domain of the mirror's border
that amuses you doubling the spaces and reversing your image?

On the other hand, seen from the visible shadow's point of view
you are the real visible shadow

Furthermore, corresponding to the different angles of vision
of your numerous I's, fragments of I's and other ghosts
      that live within you
there will be an infinite number of circumferences—worlds
with their respective 180° to the sun
   180° to the shadow
and their consequent subdomains of invisible shadows
      and mirror-shadows

All of this, no doubt, looks like Euclid's bad dream

In any case when Euclid wakes up
the monster will still be there[4]

  for Lázaro, for Esteban
  watching a Kim Ki Duk film `

De moscas y de almas

Resultan curiosas las bolsas de plástico, alargadas y transparentes
que con frecuencia cuelgan en algunos kioscos de ventas
de frutas y variedades de dulces caseros

—Exóticas frutas—digo sonriendo al ventero
—Son los mejores espantamoscas que existen—señala él—y, mientras ondea
un mugroso trapo contra las más osadas trata de explicarme el asunto

Dicho en otras palabras, la mecánica del espantamoscas es la
siguiente:

Al acercarse la mosca a la bolsa, el agua funciona como lupa invertida o espejo
deformante, el cual magnifica su tamaño hasta la desmesura. Entonces la
mosca huye aterrada de sí misma

—Así huye el alma de sus propios terrores
como mosca que lleva el diablo...
anoto, divertido

De modo sorpresivo interviene la monstruosa mosca que se ha posado en el
hombro del ventero:

O, de modo singular
en movimiento inverso a la mosca, el alma es irresistiblemente atraída fascinada ante sus terrores y en ellos se diluye o petrifica, que alguna diferencia va
de la estructura de ADN de la *Musca doméstica* o de la *Ceratitis capilata* al ser
humano...

El ventero, ocupado en la venta de un par de almojábanas,
no se da por enterado.

Yo prefiero hacer mutis por el foro como alma que lleva el diablo

Of Flies and Souls

The plastic bags are curious, elongated and see-through
frequently hanging in some fruit stands
along with various homemade sweets

—Exotic fruits—I say smiling at the shopkeeper
—They're the best fly repellent around—he replies—while waving a filthy rag
at the most daring trying to make his point

In other words, the mechanics of the fly repellent are
the following:

When the fly approaches the bag, the water functions as a loupe or
a deforming mirror that magnifies the fly's size to the point of disproportion.
Then the fly flees terrified of itself

—Likewise the soul runs away from its own fears
like a bat out of hell . . .
I note, amused

Surprisingly the monstrous fly intervenes in the conversation, sitting on the shopkeeper's shoulder:

Oddly enough
contrary to the fly the soul is hopelessly attracted, transfixed before its fears
so weakened and petrified because there's little difference between the DNA
of the domestic house fly or the *Ceratitis capitata*[6] and the DNA of the
human being . . .

The shopkeeper, occupied with a sale of a pair of *almojábanas*,[7] doesn't take
the hint.

I prefer to remain silent and make my getaway like a bat out of hell

Para Wittgenstein

El silencio no quiere ser dicho
El silencio de ninguna manera puede ser dicho
Pero acaso el silencio quisiera ser dicho
Pero acaso el silencio pudiera ser dicho
Acaso lo dicho es ya silencio
O el silencio calla disfrazado en el bullicio

Acaso el poema: todas las anteriores

al Rey Ricardo

For Wittgenstein

The silence doesn't want to be spoken
In no way can the silence be spoken
But perhaps the silence would want to be spoken
But perhaps the silence could be spoken
Perhaps the spoken is already silent
Or the silence is hushed, disguised in the noise

Perhaps the poem: all of the above

for Rey Ricardo

Poiesis

El índice de la mano derecha
se desliza en el diccionario hasta la altura
                de la palabra montaña

La mano izquierda ya fatigada de tareas
decide tomarla por un pájaro
y busca una jaula y la introduce en ella

La montaña comienza a entonar un canto dulce y pesado
                un canto de montaña

El niño cierra el diccionario
y, en visible esfuerzo, sosteniendo con ambas manos la jaula, exclama:
—mira, madre, un pájaro-montaña ¿puedo quedármelo?
—Sí, hijo, dice, como al descuido sonreída, la madre

mientras recoge algo de tierra suelta y algunas hojas húmedas

que empiezan a caer sobre la baldosa

Poiesis

The index finger of the right hand
slides in the dictionary up to the
                        word mountain

Already tired of homework the left hand
decides to take it for a bird
and looks for a cage to put it in

The mountain begins to sing a sweet and doleful song
                              a mountain song

The boy closes the dictionary
and, trying hard to hold the cage in both hands, exclaims:
—look, mother, a mountain bird, can I keep it?
—Yes, son, she says, with a careless smile,

while collecting some loose soil and wet leaves

that begin to fall on the tiled floor

Cenzontle

Pájaro numeroso el Cenzontle
Ahora es una violina
Después un azulejo, un muchacho que silba,
                    un sangretoro, un turpial
De cuatrocientos cantos habla la etimología náhuatl

Pero, a veces, pareciera cansarse
                    de ser tantos pájaros
y ensaya un misterioso silencio
Todo su adentro calla
como si se escuchara a sí mismo callando
como si descubriera que en su silencio habita otro pájaro
que canta
suspendido en su ramaje interior
Es, quizás, entonces, más cenzontle el cenzontle

    a Samuel Serrano

Cenzontle[8]

The Cenzontle bird is numerous
Now he's a violin
Then a tile, whistling boy,
        a *sangretoro*,[9] a *turpial*[10]
The Náhuatl[11] etymology speaks of four hundred songs

But, sometimes, he would appear to be tired
                of being so many birds
and he tries a mysterious silence
All inside him becomes quiet
as if he were listening to his own silence
as if he were to discover that in his silence lives another bird
that sings
sitting on its inner branch
Then, perhaps, the cenzontle is more cenzontle

    for Samuel Serrano

Tropismos

Dicen
que el girasol es una flor que ora
porque vuelve siempre su rostro hacia
                              el esplendor

Girante oración de numerosos pétalos

También he escuchado que algunas veces
el alma cegada por su propia luz
                          como en espejo
crea una flor inversa: la girasombra

Y entonces toda ella gira inmersa en ofuscación

Girasol... girasombra... girasol...

La una está, arriba, la otra está abajo
Las dos se confunden, las dos se rechazan,
Las dos son reales, las dos son irreales
Las dos son la nada, las dos son el infinito
Girasombra... girasol... girasombra

Ciertamente
Misteriosa es la flora del espíritu
Extraños los tropismos de la imaginación

Tropisms

They say
The sunflower is a flower that prays
because it always turns its face toward
                          splendor

Spinning prayer of so many petals

Also I have heard that some times
the soul is blinded by its own light
                          as in a mirror
creates a reverse flower: a sunflower-shadow

And then all turns immersed in a blur

Sunflower . . . sunflower-shadow . . . sunflower . . .

One is high, the other is low
The two confuse each other, the two reject each other,
The two are real, the two are unreal
The two are nothing, the two are infinite
Sunflower-shadow . . . sunflower . . . sunflower-shadow

Certainly
The spirit's flower is mysterious
The tropisms of the imagination are strange

Muerte y levitación de la ballena

En pausado sueño veo caer la ballena

230 toneladas de carroña o alimento cayendo
230 mundos de gravedad empujando hacia abajo
230 infinitas toneladas de vértigo
mecidas, en cámara lenta, por imperceptibles corrientes oceánicas

Inmensa, poderosamente muerta, la ballena

Pareciera que su caída suscitara el abismo
                        en que está cayendo

Como el gran mulo de Lezama va cayendo en el abismo la ballena
Como Lezama mismo
ornamentado con la majestad de todas sus grosuras va cayendo

A los 20 niveles de profundidad la ballena
                        ha perdido ya sus dos aletas

Eficaces mandíbulas lo atestiguan

Seres sin ojos la miran caer
Seres sin bocas raen su densa carne

Muchos años tomará el proceso de descarnamiento total
                                  de la ballena
hasta que al fin alcance su más recóndita blancura
Me digo en el sueño

Pero, ¿en realidad cae, está cayendo la ballena?

¿Cómo saber con certidumbre si un cuerpo está cayendo
                        sobre el mundo

o si es el mundo el que se está elevándose/cayendo
                      sobre dicho cuerpo?

Este inusual tipo de preguntas ya lo han afrontado
                algunos estudiosos de la nueva física

Menos extrañeza produce tal pregunta si las cosas ocurren
                      en un pausado sueño

Terrible, blanca ballena
lábil rastro de espuma cayente, muéstrame tu no visible belleza

Invoco sonámbulo

Y por un instante la puedo ver detenida en su caída
                        suspendida, palpitante
elevándose como asombrosa flor del abismo, en el vasto
                      esplendor del vacío

Pero, ¿en realidad, levita, está levitando la ballena?

Esto casi equivale a preguntarse, rayando los umbrales
                      del lugar común
¿Cómo saber con certidumbre cuál es el verdadero sueño
              el sueño del soñante o la vigilia del vigilante?

Talvez
todo se funde en el poder germinal de las imágenes
                    como asegura Bachelard

Es decir, el sueño vigilante, es decir, la vigilia soñante

Es decir, en fin
ese misterioso lugar donde también la ballena
pudiera vernos caer o ascender en pausado sueño

Death and Levitation of the Whale

In a dream, as if in a haze, I see the whale fall

230 tons of carrion or food falling
230 worlds of gravity pushing toward the bottom
230 infinite tons of vertigo
rocked, in slow motion, by imperceptive oceanic currents

The whale—immense, almighty dead

It would appear that its fall might raise the abyss
                                 into which it is falling

Like Lezama's great mule[12] falling into the abyss the whale
Like Lezama himself
adorned with the majesty of all its fat falling

Into the 20 levels of profundity the whale
                             has already lost its flippers

Biting jaws bear witness

Beings without eyes watch it fall
Beings without mouths scrape its dense flesh

It will take many years this tearing off all the whale's
                                         flesh
until finally it becomes the most impenetrable whiteness
I say to myself in my dream

But, is it really falling, is the whale falling?

How do you know with certainty if a body's falling
                             on the world

or if it's the world that's rising/falling
                    to the said body?

These unusual kinds of questions have already been asked
                              by some scholars of the new physics

Those questions are not so strange if the things happen
                        in a hazy dream

Terrible, white whale
labile trace of falling foam, show me your unseen beauty

I ask in my somnolence

And for an instant I can see it held in its fall
                      suspended, beating

elevating like a stunning flower of the abyss, in the vast
                        magnificence of the void

But, in reality, it levitates, is the whale rising?

This is like wondering, scraping the threshold of
                      the common place

How do we know with certainty which is the true dream
                        the dreamer's dream or the keeper's vigil?

Maybe
everything is melting in the germinal power of the images
                          as Bachelard[13] assures

That is to say, the vigilant dream, that is to say, the dreaming vigil

That is to say, finally
this mysterious place where the whale
could also see us falling or ascending in a hazy dream

Evocando a G. Bateson

La delicada estructura formada por un niño que juega, un cangrejo agazapado en su hueco y el tercer pétalo de la indecible voz de un crisantemo en el jarrón sobre el aparador. O la configurada por las sutiles redes de relaciones entre ese mismo niño, el vuelo súbito de un pájaro toche emergido entre los matorrales y la blancura de ese mismo pétalo. O la formada por el niño antípodas, al otro lado del espejo o del océano, una estrella de mar y un apagado asteroide de la constelación de Orión cuya imagen espectral aún seguiremos viendo muchos años más tarde, cuando ya no existan el niño, el crisantemo o el pensativo cangrejo ni la mano que traza esta página.

Todo eso en el preciso instante en que la frágil envoltura de la flor de tu adentro acontece

Evoking G. Bateson[14]

The delicate structure made by a child playing, a crab crouching in his hole and the third petal of the indescribable voice of a chrysanthemum in the vase on the counter. Or the one shaped by the subtle networks of relations between this same child, the subtle flight of the Andean bird emerging from bushes and the whiteness of these same petals. Or the one formed by the other child, on the other side of the mirror or of the ocean, a starfish and a burnt-out asteroid from the constellation Orion whose ghostly image we will still see many years later, when the child no longer exists, nor the chrysanthemum or the thoughtful crab nor the hand that writes on this page.

All this at the precise moment when the delicate wrapping of the flower within you begins to unfold

El fulgor

El fulgor hace parte de la vida secreta de la sombra. Hay raíz hacia abajo y raíz hacia arriba. Esto lo saben los jardineros
y, escasamente, algunos pocos teólogos. Está demostrado que no solo las plantas poseen fototropismo positivo, también ciertas zonas del alma. De hecho de ciertos místicos se ha dicho que llegaron a desarrollar, sobre el área de la coronilla, minúsculas, casi invisibles, radículas *caelum*.

El fulgor es la sombra cuando una mirada pura la mira

The Radiance

The radiance is part of the secret life of the shadow. There is a root down below and a root up above. This is what gardeners know
and, just, a few theologians. It's been proven not only do plants have positive phototropism,[15] but also certain regions of the soul. In fact, certain mystics have been said to have developed, on the crown area, miniature, nearly invisible, *caelum* radicles.[16]

The radiance is the shadow when an innocent gaze looks at it

Sufí

Como un perro que inútilmente
intenta morder su cola
giro en sentido inverso del movimiento
                                 de los astros
para alcanzar mi sombra

Sólo ella
puede darme noticias
de mi luz

Sufi

Like a dog that hopelessly
tries to bite his own tail
I spin in reverse rotation to the movement
                              of the heavenly bodies
to catch my shadow

Only it
can give me news
of my light

Escalera

Perfecciona el arte de no mirar
hasta que el blanco sea la blancura

Cierra bien la puerta
para que, al fin, el huésped
          se abra al visitante

Construye clavo a clavo una escalera
Y ya concluida
desciende por ella
y a medida que bajes
ve deshaciendo con esmero cada peldaño

Que sólo quede su fulgor ciego
su no lugar en el aire

Esto podría ser suficiente

Stairs

Refine the art of not looking
until the target becomes the whiteness

Close the door tightly
so that, finally, the host
          opens himself to the visitor

Build a stair nail by nail
And when you finish
as you come down the stairs
in the middle of your descent
neatly undo every step

So that only its radiance remains
it's nowhere in the air

This could be enough

Ilímites

En alguna fase de su galope
las cuatro patas del animal están en el aire

Por un instante la rosa de los vientos
                              abre su centro
florece en sus cuatro pétalos
y los cuatro territorios del caballo están suspendidos
por hilos de plata

En ese mínimo instante
el animal es un pájaro

Limitless

At some stage of its gallop
all four of the animal's hooves are in the air

For an instant the compass rose
                    opens its center
flowers with its four petals
and the horse's four quarters are suspended
by threads of silver

For an instant
the animal is a bird

La casa

Ahora vamos a techar la casa
Ahora vamos a sellar o abrir su último límite

Hemos cavado con firmeza sus cimientos y levantado
                               sus cuatro costados
como costillares minuciosos de un arca
Hemos empotrado y claveteado cada una de sus puertas y ventanas
y diestramente apuntalado la viga maestra

Todo esto lo hemos hecho siguiendo
las ocultas simetrías y el latido de los astros

Ahora te aguarda como su huésped

¿Pero acaso no ha sido siempre el huésped
                               la primera piedra de la casa
el punto invisible
desde el cual crecen sus orillas y muros?

¿Acaso no es la casa solo la forma
                         vacía, reverso deseante, del huésped?

Ahora estás en el centro de la casa

Y hacia cualquier lugar de la casa
                        que dirijas tus pasos
ese lugar será el centro de la casa

Ahora—lo sabes, empiezas a saberlo—
podrás desbordarte
o contraerte hasta el pequeño hueco de tu ombligo
o caer, en vértigo de cielo, sobre la palma
                             de tu mano

Ahora habitas en el centro de ti

Y podrás desplazarte por tus doce puntos cardinales
Y la casa irá contigo leve de objetos y memoria

Solo tú
Solo la casa como fluido caracol

La casa
fijada, abierta a tu ser
Sombra, deriva, resplandor
                de ti mismo

La imaginaria casa

The House

Now let's roof the house
Now let's seal or open its last limit

We have firmly dug its foundations and raised
                                            its four sides
like the flawless ribs of an ark
We have fitted and nailed each one of its doors and windows
and skillfully erected the main beam

All of this we did following
the hidden symmetries and movements of the stars

Now it awaits you as its guest

But maybe hasn't the guest always been
                                    the cornerstone of the house
the invisible point
from where its edges and walls rise?

Perhaps it's not the house, only the empty
                             form, the guest's reverse desire?

Now you are in the center of the house

And toward whichever spot in the house
                              that you direct your steps
this spot will be the house's center

Now—you know it, you start to know it—
you'll be able to spread
or shrink down to the little hole of your navel
or fall, in vertigo from the sky, on the palm
                                       of your hand

Now you live in your center

And you'll be able to move through your twelve cardinal points
And the house will go with you free of objects and memories

Only you
Only the house like a fluid snail

The house
fixed, open to your being
Shadow, adrift, your own
               brightness

The imaginary house

La pupila incesante

The Incessant Pupil

2016

Semántica del mundo

El mundo es siempre sí y no
Sino lúdico. Incongruencia. *Humor*
                cósmico
Por ejemplo
ahora voy a enrollar este texto
          que aún no es texto
Lo voy a enrollar sobre sí mismo
Sobre su sí
Sobre su no
Sobre su sino
Sobre su si no
Lo voy a enrollar sobre su signo
Para que tú
lo desenrrolles en su espejeante gnosi(s)

Semantics of the World[1]

The world is always yes and no
Fate. Inconsistent. *Cosmic*
                humor
For instance
now I'm going to roll up this text
        that still isn't a text
I'm going to roll it up on itself
On its yes
On its no
On its fate
On its if
I'm going to roll it up on its sign
So that you may
unroll it in its mirrored gnosi(s)

Ser y no ser

Puedes tener dos valvas
Eso no te hace necesariamente un molusco
si las mantienes bien abiertas

Nada hace mejor al alma
que estar oreada
que el afuera esté adentro
Así toda la extensión del ser será afuera, espacio puro
                                              del adentro

Desde luego con un ojo bien despierto en cada valva
Tampoco se puede andar por ahí con las vísceras
                                          al aire
Siendo, después de todo
quiéraslo o no, un indefenso molusco

To Be and Not to Be

You can have two valves
That doesn't necessarily make you a mollusk
if you keep them wide open

Nothing makes the soul better
than to be aired
may the outside be inside
So the total extent of the being will be outside, pure space
                                        of the inside

Certainly, with an eye on each valve
One can't walk around with the viscera
                            exposed
Being, after all
like it or not, a defenseless mollusk

Jacob y el ángel revisitados

Comprendo que no soy un perro
porque no levanto una pata trasera y orino
cuando encuentro una pared o un árbol

Comprendo que no soy un ángel
porque me dejo caer de un sexto piso
y salta en añicos mi precario vuelo

La idea de un ángel/perro, de un *ang-rro*
                    no me desagrada

Pero tan pronto la imagino, el ángel se llena de filos
y el perro confunde al ángel con un árbol
e inevitable levanta su pata

Me aturde el furor del ángel
Me paraliza su implacable pureza, su falta de piedad
Y no atrevo confrontarlo

El perro no parece inquietarse ante todo esto
y se marcha en busca de su árbol
Yo sigo sus azarosos pasos, detrás de él
                        cojeando

Jacob and the Angel Revisited[2]

I know that I'm not a dog
because I don't raise my hind leg and urinate
when I see a wall or a tree

I know that I'm not an angel
because I let myself fall from the sixth floor
and my precarious flight ends in pieces

The idea of an angel/dog, of an *ang-og*
                    doesn't bother me

But as soon as I imagine it, the angel is filled with fangs
and the dog confuses the angel with a tree
and inevitably raises his leg

I'm stunned by the angel's fury
I'm frozen by his inexorable purity, his lack of mercy
And I dare not confront him

The dog doesn't seem to be worried by any of this
and he leaves in search of his tree
I follow his random steps, behind him
                          limping

Metafísica

Después de que te has sentado
de una buena vez en el retrete
bien puedes pensar con Leibnitz
que este sea el mejor de los mundos posibles

Esta sensación de plenitud
puede durar aproximadamente entre 60
                      y 146 segundos
dependiendo, claro está, de la envergadura
                                              del asunto

Lo inquietante de todo esto
es que a lo mejor no te equivocas

Metaphysics

After you've sat
on the toilet awhile
you can think with Leibniz[3]
this may be the best of all possible worlds

This sense of fulfillment
can last between approximately 60
           and 146 seconds
depending, of course, on the scope
                                            of the matter

The disturbing thing about all of this
is that maybe you're not wrong

Poeta

Sospecha de mí

Es sano sospechar de un poeta
que ha publicado su quinto libro
Mejor aún
Sospecha a partir del segundo

Tout le rest pudiera ser literatura
Trampa
Lánguida hipoteca al oficio

Pronto habré publicado el sexto

Juro que no soy Pedro
pero ya he negado tres veces
Y aún no canta el gallo

Poet

Don't trust me

It's sane not to trust a poet
who has published his fifth book
Even better
Not to trust him after the second one

Tout le rest[4] could be literature
Trap
Halfhearted payment to the craft

Soon I will have published the sixth

I swear that I am not Peter
but I have already denied it three times
And the cock has not yet crowed

Poema de amor con serpientes, erizos y palomas

I

El camino serpeaba entre yerbajos
Me topé con dos serpientes que formaban un nudo
                                    movedizo
—Hacemos el amor
Me dijeron con sus ojos de serpiente al sentirse
                                    observadas
Yo les arrojé la camisa que llevaba puesta
No para cubrir su desnudez sino para atraparlas
Para atrapar el amor con todas sus escamas

Las metí en mi bolso de viaje

Ya tengo dos serpientes
Ahora solo me falta un paraíso, me dije
Pero cuando abrí el bolso solo hallé sus opacas
                                    mudas de piel

II

El camino se erizaba de yerbajos
Me topé con dos erizos, macho y hembra, hasta donde
                                    me fue dado saber
—Hacemos el amor
me dijeron con sus ojos de erizo cuando se sintieron
                                    observados
Y siguieron en éxtasis clavándose sus agujas

Me atraía ese amor con todas sus agujas

Pero por precaución decidí no meterlos
                   en mi bolso de viaje

III

El camino palomeaba entre yerbajos
Como supondrá el lector me topé
                        con dos palomas
que me dijeron: hacemos el amor, con sus ojos de
                                  paloma

Las metí en mi bolso de viaje

Esa noche cené caldo de palomas, por si las moscas

    a Osvaldito
    que me enseñó a atraparlas

Love Poem with Snakes, Porcupines and Doves

I

The path wound through the low grass
I ran into two snakes entwined in a wriggling
                                          knot
—We're making love
they said to me with snakes' eyes as they
                                  sensed me watching
I threw them the shirt that I was wearing
Not to cover their nudity but to catch them
To catch their love with all its scales

I put them in my travel bag

Now I have two snakes
Now all I need is a paradise, I said to myself
But when I opened the bag all I found was their colorless
                        shed skin

II

The path bristled up from the low grass
I came across two porcupines, male and female, as far as I
                        could tell
—We're making love
they said to me with porcupines' eyes as they
                                  sensed me watching
And they continued in ecstasy, sticking each other with their needles

I was drawn to their love with all its needles

But as a precaution I decided not put them
                    in my travel bag

III

The path flew through the low grass
As the reader will assume, I ran into
        two doves
that said to me: we're making love, with doves'
                eyes

I put them in my travel bag

That night I ate dove soup, just in case

    for Osvaldito
    who taught me to catch them

Poema con sombra parlante

¿Será verdad eso de nuestro *desamparo radical*
como afirman algunos?
¿Y es que tendríamos que estar acompañados?
Para compañía debiera bastarnos nuestra
                    propia sombra
Como un niño que juega marcha delante
              o detrás de mí
—o al lado—bailando ágil al ritmo de las horas
A veces se enreda en mis pies y me hace
                  perder el paso
olvidado yo de mi propio baile
Pero no lo hace de puro mala sombra
sino acaso para recordarme
que creer en un desamparo radical
comporta el mismo procedimiento imaginario
que creer en un amparo radical
Menuda sombra filosófica la mía
Y cómo habla, la muy sombra

Poem with a Talking Shadow

Is it true what they say about
our *absolute abandonment?*
Should we all be accompanied?
Because company should be our own
                              shadow
Like a child who plays while walking in front
                                     or behind me
or by my side—dancing sprightly to the rhythm of the hours
Sometimes it gets tangled up in my feet and makes me
                              lose my way
I forget my own dance
But that doesn't make it a completely bad shadow
but perhaps it's to remind me
that to believe in absolute abandonment
involves the same flight of imagination
as belief in absolute protection
What a philosophical shadow I have
And how it speaks, the very shadow

Cabeza de Medusa con espejo

El héroe se apresta con todos los atavíos
Flechas, ballesta, lanzas, redes, cuchillos ...
Y retorna con la cabeza de Medusa
convertida en trofeo

La serpiente cabeza alega
que el artero truco del espejo
la puso en desventaja
y acusa de parcialidad al enunciador lírico
pues no lo incluyó en el catálogo de armas
del segmento anterior
El enunciador decide recomenzar
e incluye el espejo y darle una variante
menos convencional al asunto

Ahora retorna Medusa con la cabeza del trofeo
convertida en héroe trágico
—pero el narrador ha olvidado cubrir con un paño la cabeza de
Medusa, como hizo la primera vez aunque no lo dijera—
Medusa entonces dirige la pavorosa mirada al narrador
y acaba limpiamente con el cuento

¿Cuento?
Pero, ¿no era esto un poema?
—arguye, en buena lógica, el lector—
(no sin antes ponerse a buen seguro pasando
         la página del texto)

Medusa's Head[5] with a Mirror

The ready hero has all his weapons
Arrow, crossbow, spear, nets, knives . . .
And he returns with the head of Medusa
now a trophy

The serpent-like head claims
that the devious trick with the mirror
put her at a disadvantage
and she accuses the poet of bias
because he didn't include it in the list of weapons
in the previous stanza
The poet decides to start again
and includes the mirror and tells a
less conventional version

Now Medusa returns with the head as a trophy
now a tragic hero
—but the narrator has forgotten to cover
Medusa's head with a cloth, as he did the first time although he didn't say so
Medusa then directs her horrible gaze at the narrator
and abruptly ends the story

Story?
But, wasn't this a poem?
—the reader argues, with good reason—
(but first makes sure to turn
        the page)

La pupila incesante

El ojo de la mosca

nunca equivoca el mejor sitio para posarse
Su revoloteo es baile sobre la mortecina

El gusano es más filosófico
prefiere trabajar en lo profundo
hasta la disolución final, ese territorio
        tan cercano al milagro
donde el miasma vuelve a ser mosca, gusano
               pétalo, ángel
o pupila incesante que contempla este juego

The Incessant Pupil

The eye of the fly

is never wrong about the best place to rest
Its flitting is a dance on carrion

The worm is more philosophical
it prefers to work deep down
until the final dissolution, this dominion
                              so close to a miracle
where the miasma transforms into a fly, worm
                                    petal, angel
or incessant pupil that contemplates this game

O viceversa

Deja que la rampa eléctrica camine por ti
Déjala hacer su trabajo
Curioso examinas con cuidado su ciclo infinito
No encierra ningún alto sentido
este juego más de la tecnología
No tengas prisa
Deja descansar tus pobres pies
siempre haciendo el fatigoso oficio
de llevarte de un destino aparente a otro

El camino que camina—te dices, observándola
en amago de ponerte trascendente

Pero, quien quita, acaso al final de la dilatada rampa
como si alguien proyectara un dorado resplandor
                              a tus espaldas
por fin halles, delante de ti, tu sombra
O viceversa

Or Vice Versa

Let the moving sidewalk walk for you
Let it do its job
Inquisitive, you carefully examine the infinite circle
It doesn't have any greater meaning
another game of technology
Don't be in a hurry
Let your poor feet rest
always doing the exhausting work
of taking you from one apparent destination to the other

The path that walks—you tell yourself, observing it
almost philosophically

But who knows maybe at the end of the moving sidewalk
as if someone were to project a golden beam of light
                              on your back
finally you find, in front of you, your shadow
Or vice versa

Bertica

Bertica bailaba en mitad de la calle
con los pies descalzos y los ojos cerrados
—¿Por qué cierras los ojos cuando bailas?—me atreví
una vez a preguntarle
—Para oír los colores de la música...
Y se quedó así, bailando
con la misteriosa belleza sin ojos de las estatuas
                                    griegas

Muchos años después Bertica se fue a vivir a uno
de mis poemas
donde aún sigue bailando con los ojos cerrados
mientras suena increíble la *Descarga Chihuahua*
Por si alguien quiere visitarla
esta es su nueva dirección:
p. 59 de *Estación de la sed*, editorial Magisterio, 1998

a Albertico, a Rosario
que también la vieron

Bertica

Bertica was dancing in the middle of the street
barefoot with her eyes closed
—Why do you close your eyes when you dance?—I dared
to ask her once
—To hear the colors of the music . . .
And she kept dancing
with the mysterious eyeless beauty of
                    Greek statues

Many years later Bertica went to live in one
of my poems
where she's still dancing with her eyes closed
while the incredible "Descarga Chihuahua"[6] plays
In case anyone wants to visit her
this is her new address:
p. 59 of *Estación de la sed*, Magisterio publisher, 1998

    for Albertico and Rosario
    who also saw her

Péndulo

El péndulo
No hace otra cosa que buscar su centro

Es extraño verlo ir hipnóticamente
de un extremo a otro

Busca la quietud
Por eso se mueve

Se busca a sí mismo
Por eso no se alcanza

a Alberto Abello

Pendulum

The pendulum
Does nothing else but look for its center

It's strange to see it going hypnotically
from one extreme to the other

It searches for stillness
For this it moves

It looks for itself
That's why it doesn't find itself

for Alberto Abello

Ceremonias

I

Una lámina de metal pulido
fulgente como un espejo. Se le hace descender por escalinatas a una
habitación oscura. La sombra no tarda en devorar toda la luz que la
habita. Así, el espejo puede liberarse del oficio de ser espejo y
dedicarse a sus propios fantasmas

II

Un ojo de agua
del que mana luz como fina arena
Asperjarlo, mirando fijamente la curva línea
del horizonte. Enderezarla con las manos.
Caminar con sumo cuidado sobre ella

III

Un cabello del canto de un pájaro
expuesto a la pupila de la luna. Verlo como relumbra
en su callada música. Hacerle un nudo
en cada uno de los extremos para sujetar ese silencio

IV

Una imposible máquina para atrapar a Dios
Algo de espejo abismal, de erizada antena fabulosa
Se escuchará solo el monstruoso bramido, el eco
el envés de su presencia

Ceremonies

I

One sheet of polished metal
glowing like a mirror. It descends the stairs into
a dark room. The darkness doesn't take long to devour all the light
that lives there. So the mirror can free itself from the business of being
a mirror and dedicate itself to its own ghosts

II

A spring
pours out light like fine sand
Sprinkle it, staring at the curved line
of the horizon. Straighten it with your hands.
Walk over it very carefully

III

A hair from a bird's song
exposed to the pupil of the moon. See it shine
in its silent music. Make a knot
at each end to hold this silence

IV

An impossible machine to trap God
Something like an enormous mirror, a wonderful bristled antenna
Only the monstrous roar will be heard, the echo
the inverse of his presence

Notes

INTRODUCTION

1. Jaramillo Agudelo, "Un collage sobre la poesía de Rómulo Bustos Aguirre," 9.
2. Valdelamar Sarabia, "Aproximación a la poesía de Rómulo Bustos," 11.
3. Santos García, "Héctor Rojas Herazo, Giovanni Quessep y Rómulo Bustos Aguirre," 85n3.
4. Santos García, "Rómulo Bustos Aguirre: La poesía como asedio del silencio," 121. This translation and all subsequent translations are our own.
5. Willy, introduction to *The Metaphysical Poets*, 1.
6. Gaviria Echavarría, "Rómulo Bustos en sus Propias Palabras," 156.
7. Valdelamar Sarabia, "Aproximación a la poesía de Rómulo Bustos," 15.
8. Santos, "Metamorfosis del vuelo," 253.
9. Gaviria Echavarría, "Rómulo Bustos en sus Propias Palabras," 159.
10. Bustos Aguirre, "El Caribe purgatorial," 221.
11. Ibid., 223.
12. Paz, prologue to *Selected Poems of Rubén Darío*, 11.
13. Santos García, "Rómulo Bustos Aguirre: La poesía como asedio del silencio," 123.
14. See Bustos Aguirre, "El Caribe purgatorial," 221–41.
15. Valdelamar Sarabia, "Aproximación a la poesía de Rómulo Bustos," 36–37.
16. Ibid., 37.
17. Ibid.
18. Ibid.
19. Ibid., 27–28.
20. Ibid., 51.
21. Gaviria Echavarría, "Rómulo Bustos en sus Propias Palabras," 155.
22. Ibid., 155.
23. Ibid., 158.
24. Ibid.
25. Moten, *In the Break*, 7.
26. Morrison, *Playing in the Dark*.
27. Gilroy, *The Black Atlantic*.
28. Hannah-Jones et al., "The 1619 Project."
29. Zapata Olivella, *Changó, the Biggest Badass*.

30. Walcott, *Omeros*.
31. Patterson, *Slavery and Social Death*, 342.
32. Santos, "Metamorfosis del vuelo," 259.
33. MacLeish, "Ars Poetica," 106–7.
34. Santos, "Metamorfosis del vuelo," 254.

EL OSCURO SELLO DE DIOS / THE DARK STAMP OF GOD

1. The figure on the face of a compass that points to the four cardinal directions, North, South, East, and West, as well as the midpoints between them (northwest, northeast, southwest, and southeast).

2. A tall, ancient Greek or Roman jar with two handles and a narrow neck.

3. An ancient Greek mythological creature with the face and breast of a woman, the body of a lion, the wings of an eagle, and the tail of a serpent. She guarded the city of Thebes, causing drought and famine until Oedipus solved her riddle. In response, she leaped off the wall to her death.

4. Black women from San Basilio de Palenque, Colombia, one of the oldest free Black settlements in the Americas and home to Palenquero, a Spanish-based creole language that incorporates several West African languages. Typically, *palenqueras* sell fruit that they carry in large washbasins on their heads.

EN EL TRASPATIO DEL CIELO / ON THE BACK PORCH OF HEAVEN

1. A tall tree with a broad trunk and a large canopy indigenous to Central and South America, also known as a Panama tree.

2. An assortment of homemade candies and pastries made from the fruit of the tamarind tree. The tamarind tree, originally from Africa, produces leguminous fruit, in which the seeds remain in the pod even when the fruit is ripe. The pulp is juicy, fleshy, and acidic, becoming sweeter and less sour as the fruit ripens.

3. Astromelia, also known as the Peruvian lily, is a vividly colored flower native to South America.

4. A tree whose name literally means "mouse killer," because of its toxic seeds and bark. It is a tropical plant often paired with coffee plants to provide shade, and often used to feed larger grazing animals.

5. A tree indigenous to South America with large, thin, pleated leaves

that are often used to hold and wrap fish and fruit and to make baskets and containers.

6. The acacia tree, originally from Africa and Australia, a tall, umbrella-shaped tree with a wide canopy. Living in deserts and tropical areas, the acacia is thorny and has small, fragrant flowers.

7. Bustos's neologism. The word's significance is largely sonic; in particular, the *ala* sound for Bustos suggests a soothing smoothness that might complement the polished stones and the sister's sense of the color yellow (Bustos, interview with the translators, April 22, 2020).

8. A stick broken from the yaya tree, known for the hardness of its wood.

9. Red angel's trumpet (*Brugmansia sanguinea*), a species of South American flowering shrub or small tree belonging to the genus *Brugmansia* of the nightshade family. For centuries, South American Indians have cultivated and used it as a hallucinogen for shamanic purposes.

10. Bustos's neologism. The word's significance is largely sonic, with an emphasis on the hissing *s* sound (Bustos, interview with the translators, April 22, 2020).

LA ESTACIÓN DE LA SED / THE SEASON OF THIRST

1. Literally translated as botany, botanist, or botanical.
2. A beach in Cartagena, Colombia, where fishermen gather to fish or to launch their boats for deeper waters.
3. Yoruba gods. They serve as the foundation of African-derived religions in the New World, including Santería and Candomblé.

SACRIFICIALES / SACRIFICIALS

1. Opal-like inner lining of mother-of-pearl.
2. *The Hammer of Witches*, the most well-known treatise on witchcraft, written in Latin by Heinrich Kramer in 1487.
3. The investigation of the ridges of the inner surfaces of the hand or foot, or the study of fingerprints.
4. A Latin phrase meaning "unto the ages" or "eternity."
5. Of or related to hunting.
6. A medium-sized pig-like animal of Central and South America.
7. Jorge Luis Borges (1899–1986), a famous Argentine writer known for his short stories and essays.
8. A category of three-dimensional solids whose faces are identical, regular polygons meeting at the same three-dimensional angles (e.g., cubes).

9. A play on the name "Marshall Berman." Berman is the author of *All That Is Solid Melts into Air* (1982). The title borrows a line from Samuel Moore's English-language translation of *The Communist Manifesto*, by Karl Marx and Friedrich Engels (1848).

10. A kind of platonic solid with twenty triangular faces.

11. The Achilles paradox attributed to the fifth century BCE Greek philosopher Zeno. In a race between Achilles and a tortoise, if the tortoise is given a slight head start, Achilles will never catch up because he will first have to reach the point at which the tortoise started, at which time the tortoise will have moved ahead, if ever so lightly, and so on and so on.

12. Héctor Rojas Herazo (1921–2002), a Colombian novelist and artist.

13. *Duino Elegies*, by Rainer Maria Rilke, a series of ten lyric poems about beauty and existential suffering.

14. Saint Lucy, the patron saint of virgins, sight, and the city of Syracuse in Sicily, often depicted holding a plate of eyes.

15. Saint Isidore of Seville, a Spanish archbishop, scholar, and major Catholic theologian of the sixth and seventh centuries known for, among other things, his *Etymologiae*, an encyclopedia including excerpts from many classical books that would have otherwise been lost.

16. A satiric essay by Francisco de Quevedo, "Gracias y desgracias de ojo del culo" (The Graces and Disgraces of the Asshole), concerning the benefits and embarrassment associated with the anus, flatulence, and defecation.

17. Friedrich Wilhelm Joseph von Schelling (1775–1854), a German philosopher of post-Kantian German idealism.

18. A multicolored primate of the Old World monkey family.

19. Sigmund Freud (1856–1939), an Austrian psychoanalyst famous for his theory of the human psyche, particularly his work on psychosexual developmental stages.

20. Georges Bataille (1897–1962), a French writer and poet concerned with eroticism, mysticism, and the irrational.

21. Saint Catherine of Alexandria, a virgin martyr from the early fourth century.

MUERTE Y LEVITACIÓN DE LA BALLENA / DEATH AND LEVITATION OF THE WHALE

1. Refers to the study of plane and solid figures based on theorems and axioms by the Greek mathematician Euclid.

2. Roberto Juarroz (1925–1995), an Argentine poet famous for his philosophical poetic style.

3. Luis Vidales (1904–1990), the first Colombian poet to write in a strictly avant-garde style.

4. A quotation from Augusto Monterroso's famous short story "El dinosaurio" (The Dinosaur).

5. Kim Ki Duk (b. 1960), a South Korean filmmaker known for his idiosyncratic art-house works.

6. The Latin name for the Mediterranean fruit fly, best known as an extremely damaging fruit pest. Though "capilata" appears in the original Spanish, the correct spelling in Latin is "capitata."

7. Colombian cheese bread made from *cuajada* cheese and corn flour.

8. The Aztec word for mockingbird.

9. A small red and black bird indigenous to South America.

10. The national bird of Venezuela, with a long tail, bulky bill, and black head and breast contrasted with orange on its back. In English, it is called the troupial, which is a kind of New World oriole in the blackbird family.

11. The indigenous Aztec language.

12. José Lezama Lima (1910–1976), a Cuban novelist, essayist, and poet. Lezama wrote "Rapsodia para el mulo" (Rhapsody for the Mule), a contemplation of a mule's fall into an abyss.

13. Gaston Bachelard (1884–1962), a French philosopher known for his contributions to poetics and the philosophy of science.

14. Gregory Bateson (1904–1980), an English anthropologist known for his work on cultural symbolism, culture and personality, and his argument for human consciousness living in harmony with nature.

15. The orientation of a plant toward a light source.

16. A Latin word referring to a small constellation in the southern sky, meaning "chisel," or "to the sky" or "heavens."

LA PUPILA INCESANTE / THE INCESSANT PUPIL

1. The poem in Spanish plays on the words "sí" (yes) and "no" (no) to form the word "sino" (which can mean either the conjunction "but" or the noun "fate").

2. In Genesis 32:23–33, Jacob wrestles with a mysterious man (i.e., the Angel) who, while trying to beat him, dislocates Jacob's hip; Jacob still wins, refusing to let the man go until he blesses him, thus his new name, Israel.

3. Gottfried Wilhelm Leibniz (1646–1716), a German Enlightenment philosopher, logician, and mathematician who developed differential and integral calculus. The misspelling "Leibnitz" appears in the original Spanish.

4. A French phrase meaning "all the rest."

5. A monster of Greek and Roman mythology. According to Ovid, after Medusa was raped by Poseidon in Athena's temple, Athena cursed her to have snakes for hair and for the sight of her face to turn one to stone. The hero, Perseus, defeated her by using a mirror to use Medusa's powers against her, then beheaded her, gifting Medusa's head to Athena for her shield.

6. A song by the Chihuahua All Stars, led by Osvaldo "Chihuahua" Martínez. Descarga is a Cuban genre of improvisatory music using variations of Cuban musical themes and heavily influenced by American jazz.

Additional Reading

Andrews, George Reid. *Afro-Latin America: Black Lives, 1800–2000*. Cambridge, MA: Harvard University Press, 2016.

Branche, Jerome C., ed. *Black Writing, Culture, and the State in Latin America*. Nashville: Vanderbilt University Press, 2015.

———. *The Poetics and Politics of Diaspora: Transatlantic Musings*. London: Taylor and Francis, 2014.

Davis, Darién J., ed. *Beyond Slavery: The Multilayered Legacy of Africans in Latin America and the Caribbean*. Lanham, MD: Rowman and Littlefield, 2006.

Dixon, Kwame, and John Burdick, eds. *Comparative Perspectives on Afro-Latin America*. Gainesville: University Press of Florida, 2012.

Fuente, Alejandro de la, and George Reid Andrews, eds. *Afro-Latin American Studies: An Introduction*. Cambridge: Cambridge University Press, 2018.

Gudmundson, Lowell, and Justin Wolfe, eds. *Blacks and Blackness in Central America: Between Race and Place*. Durham, NC: Duke University Press, 2010.

Helg, Aline. *Liberty and Equality in Caribbean Colombia, 1770–1835*. Chapel Hill: University of North Carolina Press, 2004.

Jackson, Richard L. *The Black Image in Latin American Literature*. Albuquerque: University of New Mexico Press, 1976.

———. *Black Literature and Humanism in Latin America*. Athens: University of Georgia Press, 1988.

———. *Black Writers and Latin America: Cross-Cultural Affinities*. Washington, DC: Howard University Press, 1998.

———. *Black Writers and the Hispanic Canon*. New York: Twayne Publishers, 1997.

Jiménez Román, Miriam, and Juan Flores, eds. *The Afro-Latin@ Reader: History and Culture in the United States*. Durham, NC: Duke University Press, 2010.

LaRosa, Michael J., and Germán R. Mejía. *Colombia: A Concise Contemporary History*. Lanham, MD: Rowman and Littlefield, 2013.

Lewis, Marvin A. *Treading the Ebony Path: Ideology and Violence in Contemporary Afro-Colombian Prose Fiction*. Columbia: University of Missouri Press, 1987.

Lipski, John. *A History of Afro-Hispanic Language: Five Centuries, Five Continents*. Cambridge: Cambridge University Press, 2005.

Luis, William. *Voices from Under: Black Narrative in Latin America and the Caribbean*. Westport, CT: Greenwood Press, 1984.

Maddox, John T., IV. *Challenging the Black Atlantic: The New World Novels of Zapata Olivella and Gonçalves*. Lewisburg, PA: Bucknell University Press, 2020.

Minority Rights Group. *No Longer Invisible: Afro-Latin Americans Today*. London: Minority Rights Publications, 1995.

Moore, Carlos, Tanya R. Sanders, and Shawna Moore, eds. *African Presence in the Americas*. Trenton, NJ: Africa World Press, 1995.

Oliveira, Emanuelle K. F. *Writing Identity: The Politics of Contemporary Afro-Brazilian Literature*. West Lafayette, IN: Purdue University Press, 2010.

Restall, Matthew, ed. *Beyond Black and Red: African-Native Relations in Colonial Latin America*. Albuquerque: University of New Mexico Press, 2005.

Rout, Leslie B., Jr. *The African Experience in Spanish America, 1502 to the Present Day*. Cambridge: Cambridge University Press, 1976.

Sartre, Jean-Paul. *Being and Nothingness: A Phenomenological Essay on Ontology*. Translated by Hazel Estella Barnes. New York: Washington Square Press, 1992.

Tillis, Antonio D., ed. *Critical Perspectives on Afro-Latin American Literature*. New York: Routledge, 2012.

Torres, Arlene, and Norman E. Whitten Jr., eds. *Blackness in Latin America and the Caribbean*. 2 vols. Bloomington: Indiana University Press, 1998.

Yelvington, Kevin A., ed. *Afro-Atlantic Dialogues: Anthropology in the Diaspora*. Santa Fe, NM: School of American Research Press, 2006.

Works Cited

Bustos Aguirre, Rómulo. *Casa en el aire*. Valencia, Spain: Editorial Pre-Textos, 2017.

———. "El Caribe purgatorial: Héctor Rojas Herazo o la imaginación del fuego." In *Respirando el Caribe: Memorias de la cátedra del Caribe Colombiano*, vol. 1, edited by Ariel Castillo Mier, 221–40. Bogotá: Observatorio del Caribe Colombiano, 2001.

———. *El oscuro sello de Dios*. Bogotá: Fundación Cultural Héctor Rojas Herazo, 1988.

———. *En el traspatio del cielo*. Bogotá: Instituto Colombiano de Cultura, 1993.

———. *La estación de la sed*. Bogotá: Cooperativa Editorial Magisterio, 1998.

———. *La pupila incesante: Obra poética 1988–2013*. Bogotá: Fondo de Cultura Económica, 2016.

———. *Lunación del amor*. Cartagena, Colombia: Ediciones en Tono Menor, 1990.

———. *Muerte y levitación de la ballena*. Cali, Colombia: Universidad del Valle, 2010.

———. *Obra poética*. Bogotá: Ministerio de Cultura, 2010.

———. *Palabra que golpea un color imaginario*. Palos de la Frontera, Spain: Universidad Internacional de Andalucía, 1996.

———. *Sacrificiales*. Medellín, Colombia: Frailejón Editores, 2007.

Gaviria Echavarría, María Isabel. "Rómulo Bustos en sus Propias Palabras." *Estudios de Literatura Colombiana*, no. 39 (July–December 2016): 155–60.

Gilroy, Paul. *The Black Atlantic: Modernity and Double Consciousness*. Cambridge, MA: Harvard University Press, 1993.

Hannah-Jones, Nikole, et al. "The 1619 Project." Special issue, *New York Times Magazine*, August 14, 2019.

Jaramillo Agudelo, Darío. "Un collage sobre la poesía de Rómulo Bustos Aguirre." In *La pupila incesante: Obra poética, 1988–2013*, 9–42. 2nd ed. Cartagena, Colombia: Editorial Universitaria, 2016.

MacLeish, Archibald. "Ars Poetica." In *Collected Poems, 1917–1982*, 106–7. Boston: Houghton Mifflin, 1985.

Morrison, Toni. *Playing in the Dark: Whiteness and the Literary Imagination*. New York: Vintage, 1993.

Moten, Fred. *In the Break: The Aesthetics of the Black Radical Tradition*. Minneapolis: University of Minnesota Press, 2003.

Patterson, Orlando. *Slavery and Social Death: A Comparative Study*. Cambridge, MA: Harvard University Press, 1982.

Paz, Octavio. Prologue to *Selected Poems of Rubén Darío*, 7–18. Austin: University of Texas Press, 1965.

Santos, Emiro Rafael. "Metamorfosis del vuelo: (Im)posibilidad cognitiva y movilidad simbólica en la poesía de Rómulo Bustos Aguirre." *Mitologías Hoy* 15 (June 2017): 243–61.

Santos García, Emiro. "Héctor Rojas Herazo, Giovanni Quessep y Rómulo Bustos Aguirre: Visitando los bosques del Paraíso." *Estudios de Literatura Colombiana*, no. 36 (January–June 2015): 81–100.

———. "Rómulo Bustos Aguirre: La poesía como asedio del silencio." Interview, in *Rómulo Bustos Aguirre: Poesía escogida*, 115–27. Cartagena, Colombia: Leer el Caribe, 2014.

Sartre, Jean-Paul. "The Humanism of Existentialism." In *Essays in Existentialism*. Edited by Wade Baskin, 31–62. Secaucus, NY: Citadel Press.

Valdelamar Sarabia, Lázaro. "Aproximación a la poesía de Rómulo Bustos." Master's thesis, Universidad Andina Simón Bolívar, 2002.

Walcott, Derek. *Omeros*. New York: Noonday Press, 1990.

Willy, Margaret. Introduction to *The Metaphysical Poets*, edited by Margaret Willy, 1–11. Columbia: University of South Carolina Press, 1971.

Zapata Olivella, Manuel. *Changó, the Biggest Badass*. Translated by Jonathan Tittler. Lubbock: Texas Tech University Press, 2010.

www.ingramcontent.com/pod-product-compliance
Lightning Source LLC
Chambersburg PA
CBHW022111150426
43195CB00008B/364